W9-ARE-225

BLACK BELONGING

Contributions in Sociology
Series Editor: *D O N   M A R T I N D A L E*
University of Minnesota

---

contributions in sociology 7

Jack C. Ross

Raymond H. Wheeler

BLACK BELONGING

A STUDY OF THE SOCIAL CORRELATES OF WORK RELATIONS AMONG NEGROES

Greenwood Publishing Corporation
Westport, Connecticut

GP

Library of Congress Catalog Card Number: 77–105974
SBN: 8371–3298–3 (cloth)
SBN: 8371–5962–8 (paper)

Greenwood Publishing Corporation
51 Riverside Avenue, Westport, Connecticut 06880

Printed in the United States of America

CONTENTS

TABLES

PREFACE

One of the most consistently noted features of membership in voluntary associations is its association with occupation and other indicators of social status. Little, however, has been done to explore why occupation is related to membership in voluntary associations, other than to claim that status is the underlying factor. We have attempted to go beyond this claim by asking what features of occupation promote, induce, compel, discourage, or prevent such membership. Particular attention has been directed to the social arrangements generated by, or characteristic of, particular occupations.

An attempt at a theoretical statement of this position is presented in chapter 1 and the remaining chapters explore these issues with survey research data.

A number of persons have supplied valuable assistance. Bruce Cameron helped us at many points with timely discussions, encouragement, and penetrating criticism. Colleagues Ronald Burton and Louis Kutcher also made helpful suggestions. Nathaniel Crook, former Director of the Tampa Urban League, assisted in a variety of ways for which we are grateful. Dewey Gaddis performed admirably as our chief research assistant. Miss Marjorie Mayes proved invaluable as a major interviewer and provided liaison with other interviewers.

The National Science Foundation provided the funds (under contract GS-1395) for the major part of this study.

_____ BLACK BELONGING

1

WORK AND BELONGING: AN OVERVIEW AND A THEORY

It is the major contention of this study that social relations at a person's place of work are of decisive importance in determining his participation in the voluntary associations of his community. We will show that social relations at work are related not only to the extent of participation in, but also to the kind of associations to which the worker belongs. In testing this thesis we develop three new concepts: coracialism, reinforcement, and collegiality.

By voluntary association we mean a formal organization, small or large, in which membership is optional; that is, without compulsion or ascription. By this definition we exclude unions, which often have an aspect of compulsion, and churches, because they often are ascriptive and therefore not strictly voluntary associations. Where a more inclusive and general definition is meant, we will refer specifically to the unmodified term *association*.

In focusing on the work that Negroes in a southern U.S. city perform, we demonstrate the importance of fellow workers and supervisors in determining what people believe and what they do in their home communities. Work is the crucible; community life is one of its products. The inferior positions that Negroes occupy in most work settings make them especially sensitive to social relations, responsive to pressures to join or not join certain groups, and for sociological purposes, ideally representative of a theme basic to American life: work is a decisive determinant of what people think, feel, and do.

The approach is the synthesis of several kinds of sociological investigation. First, four years of periodic involvement on the part of the authors and their students in the life of the six Negro communities of Tampa, Florida provided insights and information that have been used to explain Negroes' involvement in community life. Second, we have conducted three survey research projects in the same area based on samples of 256, 1,100, and 1,086, the last of which is reported in the chapters which follow. Third, the comparison of our research with the accumulated knowledge in related fields has produced a theoretical approach that offers promise for understanding the relationship between work and voluntary associations beyond those examined in this specific investigation.

SOURCES FOR
A THEORY OF WORK
AND VOLUNTARY ASSOCIATIONS

The study of voluntary associations has played an important part in the development of sociology, as have voluntary associations themselves in the growth of American society. In spite of the consideration given voluntary associations, knowledge of their functions is limited and theory on the subject nearly sterile. There appear to be reasons for this lack of growth.

First, voluntary associations are an obvious element in the study of communities, consequently most monographs on communities include a section on such organizations.[1] Community studies, however, display the difficulties encountered by the functional anthropological works from which they spring: they do not easily yield any general theory that can be further applied and tested. Studies proliferate, but theory does not.

Second, these studies seem to be preoccupied with unimportant questions. For example, the idea that Americans are "joiners," derived from de Tocqueville's masterpiece, has been examined many times.[2] Refuting such clichés should hardly be the preoccupation of a maturing academic discipline. This kind of research, if it has done nothing else, has exhibited its own inner deficiency, and, predictably, has ended in quibbles about the merits of particular survey methods. Another preoccupation has been the question of whether or not Negroes are "exaggerated Americans." This notion was first considered by Gunnar Myrdal in *An American Dilemma* and has been pursued to no important conclusion.

Third, research on voluntary associations has trapped research workers in difficult methodological questions. It is easy to ask simple questions on how many associations a person belongs to—it has become as commonplace as asking about education or occupation. But to ascertain either the meaning or the causes of membership and participation has proven much more elusive. We even lack agreement on a common definition of membership. Consequently, a proliferation of gratuitous data has impeded progress. Moreover, there seems to be general acceptance of the idea that establishing a number indicative of the frequency of voluntary association membership for a category of people is in itself meritorious. The number is somehow viewed as a real indicator of social interaction. This kind of abstracted empiricism seems to have led to the concluson that methods of research are the main issue —a conclusion we reject.

Related to this third problem is a fourth: the assumption that social class is a unitary phenomenon causally related to rates of membership in voluntary associations.[3] The problem arises because of failure to distinguish the numerous ways in which social evaluations are stabilized in stratification systems; and, further, what the relationship of various kinds of associations are to each system. To follow Max Weber's terminology, the relations of class, status, and power in stable systems tend to become consistent in many cases, but there is no certainty that this will be the result in any particular social unit. Furthermore, it is proper to assume that membership in voluntary associations is one of the primary ways that "status honor" (prestige) is claimed, displayed, validated, stabilized, and transmitted. This is quite the reverse of the assumption that status causes membership. And, while associational life is crucial in the "market situation" (which for Weber is the basis of class), both associations and voluntary associations are involved in the polity, and voluntary associations frequently predominate in status-honor evaluations. A total representation of all the complexities involved would call for a comprehensive model. Our goal is more limited: we want to explain the relationship of work and membership to voluntary associations.

The reification of status and class has resulted in a deficiency of research at a vital point. Important studies of voluntary associations have been deficient because occupation has typically been used as an indicator of social class rather than as a clue to the nature of the work conditions that directly affect participation in community voluntary associations. We shall demonstrate that social relations of work are far more important, more complex, and more decisive than mere social-class level as indicated by some measure of status.

Our decision to orient this study around voluntary associations is arbitrary. Such membership information as might be shown to be the result of work-related variables by no means exhausts the subject of work. There are, in addition, continually emerging community alternatives to voluntary associations, some of which may prove to be of yet greater significance in human relationships. Moreover, researchers may discover a great deal about the consequence of social relations in the work situation at about the time work becomes less crucial in our lives. Or, to come closer to present hard facts, if, for the Negro male, the family becomes a voluntary association, or the voluntary association becomes a family, what is the significance of research like ours? We will have to bypass this consideration as being outside our major focus, pausing only to mention stimulating implications of our findings wherever they occur.

Let us now turn from criticism to a consideration of the kind of knowledge that seems most promising for constructing a theory of Negroes' work and membership in voluntary associations.

NEGROES' WORK, VOLUNTARY ASSOCIATIONS, AND MASS SOCIETY

The connection between economic enterprise and membership in voluntary associations is recognized by many businesses. In some cases, business attempts to exert control over communities, to provide them with leadership, or to influence employees' use of leisure. Litwak has shown that some corporations require certain executives to participate in local associations.[4] In another study it was found that employees of a bank were required to participate in local activities.[5] The participation of small businessmen in service, fraternal, and civic organizations is well known.

Another kind of relation between work and associations concerns unions. Although the union cannot in most cases be considered a truly voluntary association, the example of unions may be considered in formulating a theory. Spinrad's excellent summary of correlates of union membership will be used as a source of insight.[6]

When we turn our attention from a general consideration of voluntary associations to the voluntary associations of
Negroes, the utility of the few available sources diminishes.
Because of the very considerable difference between the work
of Negroes and whites, the information about community
participation of whites cannot be used, except in the most
general way, to predict the participation of Negroes.[7] For
example, an informant in Tampa, a Negro social worker,
claimed that there was no Negro employer in the entire city
who hired more than five employees. This is true if we exclude educational and welfare institutions, most of which are
controlled by whites even when they are under Negro administration. A Negro-owned newspaper hires twenty Negroes.
Furthermore, where Negroes are employees they are often
wage rather than salaried workers, and they frequently work
as sole employees (e.g., domestic workers). Also, Negroes
become white-collar workers less often than whites. Many
other distinctions could be made, but the research issue is
clear: even the limited studies on the relation of work to
voluntary association membership of whites cannot be used
to construct a theory for Negro participation. We must turn,
therefore, to other sources for suggestions about the relationship between the work and the participation of Negroes.
From an examination of the literature, we found the idea
of the contrast between a mass society and a pluralist society
a useful starting point.

"Mass society" refers to social relations that feature
minimal group involvement and social atomization. Rose
sees the mass society metaphorically as a kind of audience,
an extreme example of which is a movie theater in which
an aggregate of people simultaneously receive the same stimuli

but do not directly interact either with the source or with each other.[8] Kornhauser notes that "mass society is a social system in which elites are accessible to influence by nonelites and nonelites are readily accessible to influence by elites."[9] The man in mass society is preoccupied with "proximate concerns" and lacks involvement in "intermediate structures" such as voluntary associations, local government, and economic enterprises.

The Kerner report on civil disorders documents this lack of participation of Negroes in city government in twenty 1967 riot cities of which our research city, Tampa, was one.[10] Tampa has no Negroes in elective posts and very few in administration.[11] Our later chapters will document the infrequent participation in voluntary associations by Negroes who are self-employed. This category includes the independent businessman who is often the mainstay of local organizational life in white society. Other relevant information is lacking, such as amount of stock ownership and other forms of potential economic control. However, Negroes in Tampa recently organized a bank, and there are several mutual-aid and insurance associations, burial associations, and the like, which are well established. We do not, therefore, have a case of pure isolation from associational life, but it should be noted that much of Negro involvement in such relationships is confined to the limits of the Negro community. We are not assuming, then, that Tampa is a pure example of mass society —the idea of mass society is only a sensitizing concept used to develop a theory.

Pluralist society, by contrast with mass society, is characterized by the low availability of nonelites and high availability of elites.[12] The pluralist society involves a network of voluntary associations and other types of organizations in a complex interaction involving both conflict and cooperation. The pluralist society is dynamically stable, not easily mobilized to direct action by or against elites. However, men in a mass society act directly in relation to elites through mass movements, and are susceptible to mobilization by either charismatic or authoritarian leaders.[13] The perfect model of a mass society has alternate civic statuses: apathy and extreme activity.

It is commonplace to assert that Americans are a nation of joiners, and simultaneously to aver that Americans suffer from anomie or alienation. As is often the case with generalizations, both assertions are true in part. The fact is that the range of participation in American society runs from the complete absence of membership in voluntary associations for a great many citizens to a dozen memberships or more for a much smaller number of people. It is therefore necessary to amend Kornhauser's analysis by pointing out that it is the elite who belong to the greater number of organizations and are influential and active members. This supports the idea of a diffuse elite or power structure that is effective and influential precisely because its leadership is exerted through many affiliations.[14]

We have shown through a variety of examples that both mass and pluralist tendencies exist in American society and in Tampa. Our theoretical problem therefore is to *identify the concrete conditions under which pluralism arises.* Let us take the following statement as a provisional theory: The decisive issue is *whether the individual through his employment is effectively exposed to social relationships that support participation.* These relationships may take the form of a direct and imperative linkage of work and voluntary association. For example, the teacher is expected to join the PTA; the undertaker is expected to be a leader and contributor to the church. These verge on the nonvoluntary, but more typically we will find situations in which norms developed in a social relationship operate less directly to influence joining or to recruit people who hold value orientations appropriate to joining.

In the place of work, task differentiation gives rise to a need for social integration strong enough to coordinate the behavior of workers to the achievement of imperative ends. This will be the general assumption guiding our inquiry. Since the formal and informal factors of work that produce social integration may be associated with a variety of pluralistic consequences, we must identify those work factors which relate only to voluntary association membership. Voluntary association membership is, of course, but one consequence of the life-organizing tendency of work. And, to turn attention to the dependent variable, to predict with no systematic error the amount and type of voluntary association membership, causal factors other than work-related ones must be considered.

Without ignoring these other factors in the family and community that influence joining (we will treat them as statistical controls), we shall feature three social relationships of work; reinforcement, coracialism, and collegiality. The basic definitions are: *coracialism,* work with other Negroes; *reinforcement,* the workers' ability to call upon extrasystemic force in work; *collegiality,* work-related friendship. In addition we shall make frequent use of the concept of *authority,* defined as legitimated ability to obtain compliance.[15]

(These and other special definitions are summarized in the Glossary.)

Reinforcement and authority are readily identified as formal or the result of a contractual relationship: coracialism and collegiality, as informal. The most significant normative force on the worker consists of the formal authority of the organization (corporation, firm, bureaucracy, and so on). Coracialism, collegiality, and reinforcement ordinarily operate in complex ways against or in accommodation with authority. We are not yet ready to state what the results of these relationships will be for voluntary association memberships. We can say only that the amount and kind of membership is related to these social organizational factors of work.

SOCIAL RELATIONSHIPS AND NEGRO OCCUPATIONS

In this section we will go into considerable descriptive detail about the social relationships of work in order to indicate concrete instances of our abstract terms and variations in their occurrence. The examination is ordered by a system similar to the standard Edwards categories of the social status of work, beginning with low status.

Welfare, Unemployed, and Illegitimate Occupations

Regarding this category the basic question for our present research is whether lack of participation in work groups that are tied to legitimated and stable economic institutions restricts joining.

For the unemployed, social workers or welfare agency representatives may in part replace the employer as the source of authority over the client's community life, but their control is minimal regarding voluntary associational participation.

Included in this category of work is the set that Matza calls the "disreputable poor."[16] There are, to be sure, disreputable occupations in Negro communities that do not involve poverty, as Drake and Cayton point out.[17] It is not likely that the survey research described in this book will reveal the structure of such illegitimate occupations. We shall have to assume that random survey research contacts with the illegitimate occupations simply do not result in good data, and that the research results are thereby rendered inaccurate.[18]

Unemployment is an inclusive concept. Important at this point is that social relations are differentially altered by the meaning of the unemployment. For example, a union mason who expects periodic unemployment may find his informal relations unimpeded by a layoff. His employment is cut off, but his source of reinforcement is unaltered. For others, unemployment may involve a continued unsuccessful search for work that results in the erosion of relationships. The type of unemployment is quite important in this research: numerically, almost all of our unemployed are manual or unskilled workers for whom joblessness is critical.

Unskilled Occupations

This set consists of domestics, mass-production or assembly-line workers, isolated menials, and blue-collar entrepreneurs. In this large category we find a wide range of variation in

informal and formal relations, ranging from the highly personal relations of domestic workers with the housewife-
employers based on community norms, to the impersonal and
alienating formal authority of the factory, to the autonomy
and isolation of the blue-collar entrepreneur. Here is an
emphatic reason for rejection of a simplistic occupational
status theory of membership prediction.

Domestic work usually involves single Negroes at work
in the homes of whites, or sometimes of wealthy Negroes.[19]
The work thus is typically low in coracialism, by our definition.
Furthermore, the people with whom interaction takes place
are not of the same status, by predetermined community
standards. Regulation of behavior is influenced by tradition.
In the modern Southern city, Negro women who work for
white housewives on a part-time basis may have as many as
a dozen more-or-less regular employers. Organization of car
pools is a frequent source of social life among Negro women.
Thus the Negro doing "day's work" (colloquial for the U.S.
Department of Labor "day work") may experience less isolation from society (i.e., she does have collegiality) than those
who work as full-time maids or family employees (for males,
"yardmen") and who reside in wealthy homes (an increas-
ingly rare situation).[20] On the other hand, the employer's
formal authority over the day worker lacks continuity and
a typical sanction is simply not rehiring or refusal to give
a recommendation to another employer. Reinforcement is virtually nonexistent. Entrance into the occupation is easy—
typically by sponsorship of friends. Thus, the occupation often
serves for girls as an entrance into the world of work, while
for older women it is a flexible occupation readily fitted into
a life pattern filled with variation, contingency, and demand.

In most classifications, domestics are grouped with service

employees. However, service employees, who may be semi-skilled, often work in businesses organized for profit, and sometimes in large-scale organizations. Their social relations may be quite different from those of day workers, even though their objective status level is similar.

There are many kinds of menial work in which the laborer is isolated from socially meaningful contact, although he may interact with others as part of his job. We cannot begin to describe them all and merely to classify them as miscellaneous would do a disservice to research. The main issue is that the community and organizational definition of work as Negro work implies moral inferiority of the job, and that an inferior job is held by an inferior person. Most menial and service employees fall under such a label: orderlies, trash and garbage handlers (not in crews), charwomen, and aides who do other people's dirty work. They may be physically in the presence of superior others, but socially encapsulated or isolated. Domestics may be encapsulated because they are privy to the underlife of prestigious persons: their excretions, their trash and clutter, the symbols of their prestige—disconferring backstage and understage behavior. Domestics do have the power to ruin the scene for the housewife who seeks to use them as prestige signs, and hence they have some power to embarrass or to blackmail. Menials who are employed by organizations are not so often in direct contact with the scenes in which prestige is displayed, and in fact their drab and physically functional uniforms exhibit this value. In the more extreme case, the key criteria of moral inferiority of such nonperson status is that we talk about the person in his presence as if it doesn't matter whether or not he is there; with the very same person fickle conversation and superficially friendly association may be carried on precisely because it is well understood that nothing serious will ever be discussed, nor will mutually known normative limits be exceeded. Peasants are fun. Southern whites' patronizing illusion that they know Negroes very well is born of this pseudomutuality.

Mass production is the classical Marxian example of the source of alienation. The pure case in which the individual tends a machine and does not interact at all with others (the Charlie Chaplin role in *Modern Times*) is not as common as is often assumed. In addition, the pertinacity with which people will develop informal relations in order to make work "human" is often underestimated. Such interaction arises informally among workers in relationship to, or as escape from their work, and among supervisors who are alienated in their own ways and at their own level. The union, where present, is a source of reinforcement. While theoretically important as a kind of normative development and anonymity, it is not important in this particular research because of the relative absence in Tampa of the type of industry in which it occurs.

A large number of manual workers do heavy physical work, frequently as members of a gang. The individuals are essentially interchangeable so far as skill is concerned, and the division of labor is minimal. Collegiality is usually possible, although the impermanence of the work may limit the growth of strong friendships. Reinforcement is often through a union, although many Negro manual workers are not unionized. Coracialism is usually present due to racial homogeneity of work gangs, but since task differentiation of the job, where it occurs, is usually along racial lines with Negroes doing the undesirable part, Negroes are in a constant state of subordination on the basis of race.[21]

The blue-collar entrepreneur is a dilemma for the classifier of social status. On the one hand, he shares in the honored American dream to be his own boss, and to have a little place of his own. In this sense he would be classified as a proprietor, next to the top of the Edwards' scale. On the other hand, the work he does is simple and might best be classified as unskilled or semiskilled and with appropriate low status. In our approach we do not rely on the effects of his status, but on his social relations, and so we must examine his actual work routines and practices. Blue-collar entrepreneurs, such as itinerant peddlers of cheap products, yard workers with their own equipment, door-to-door solicitors of odd jobs, car junkers, at-home launderers, and so on, have similar patterns. They form few structured and permanent relationships with their clients. Their recourse from abrasive white norms is their ability to abandon the present job and to go on to another. Thus they are not constrained by formal authority. Among Negroes, blue-collar entrepreneurship is a way that an outcast person can gain a sense of freedom and dignity, however limited and subject to the consequences of status inconsistency. In sum, he experiences neither reinforcement nor authority, and whatever collegiality occurs is due to his casual proximity to other people in the course of his work.

Semiskilled

This set consists of operatives, service workers, and normative independent task workers. In the case of normative independent task workers, single Negroes work among whites or other Negroes performing repetitive or production tasks not at the mass production level. Their tasks are so differentiated that they require low-level decision making and interaction coordinated with other workers, white or Negro. A task is defined here as a unit of production in which a worker performs or controls a series of operations that are related to other operations. The work allows for the identification of responsibility for performance as to the quality and quantity of the product, leading to enduring evaluation of the person or the groups of which he is a member, and a subsequent emergence of status levels. Typical jobs would include freight-handling, laundry plant work, food-processing, product-packing, and operating simple, nonautomatic machines.

One of the unique features of our point of departure emerges here. The same description given above (of blue-collar normative task workers) applies as well to some work usually listed as white-collar.[22] One of the confusing aspects of research on voluntary associations is that it is simply assumed that at all levels participation is higher among white-collar workers than blue-collar workers because this is empirically true in general. We think the issue is social relations of the job, rather than the requirements of white-collar status alone. We must therefore also include in this category such white-collar or gray-collar jobs (involving the right to a desk and comfort perquisites) as order-filling and various simple clerical tasks. These are white-collar production workers who may have sought-after statuses that support more elegant presentation of the person, the desired comfort of station, and the status of paper worker, but who nevertheless do not encounter in their work any more norms that support participation in voluntary associations than do blue-collar workers. As the examples in the later chapters will reveal, Negro white-collar workers of this kind are relatively few in the research city, while blue-collar production workers are very prevalent.

Operatives are people who control machines. Among the most common are drivers and operators of construction equipment. Service workers, another semiskilled category, frequently use simple machines, but with skills limited to those acquired in the home or in technical schools and applied in personal or institutional service. They are trained rather than educated. Negro women are frequently found as nurses' aides, beauticians, and the like; Negro men as barbers, porters, and stewards. These may have much in common with independent task workers, but they frequently work alone or in small shops. Authority over the worker may vary greatly, due to the power or worth of the machine or product and the potential damage of its misuse. Collegiality may be limited due to lack of opportunity for contact, and reinforcement typically is through the union or civil service.

We now move to occupations that are classified as white-collar on the Edwards' scale.

Clerical Workers

It was noted above that Negro clerical and sales workers are rare in Tampa. Many of them are, in fact, normative independent task workers. The category is a broad one, however, ranging from salesgirls and stenographers to insurance salesmen with considerable technical knowledge. Clerical and sales work is sociologically distinguished by the fact that it involves a high level of detail and specification, and frequently a complex division of labor, under authority which is necessary to accomplish integration of tasks with other parts of the enterprise. Standardized products involved are handled in standard ways and subordinated to managerial judgment. The individual frequently becomes a standard representative (or agent of the enterprise) to customers and, therefore, personal presentations become a part of standardized technical performance. Ultimately, the person becomes the technique. Authority then extends to personal relations and the informal relations may become subtle and intricate. Reinforcement typically is from civil service rather than from unions. White-controlled businesses in the South rarely choose a Negro as a representative in such cases. A Negro is assumed to be categorically déclassé in personal relations with whites and does not typically confer status on the organization represented. The day of the Negro organization man has yet to come to most of the South.

Farmers

In more detailed studies than ours, farmers might be further classified as owners, managers, laborers, and so on, according to various specialties. In our research a few city-dwelling farm laborers appeared in the sample and are listed in the appropriate blue-collar category. There was but one owner of a farm in the sample.

Managers, Proprietors, and Officials

Of this set, only proprietors are found in significant numbers in Tampa, due to the small size of Negro businesses and the discriminatory conditions in white firms. Where a distinction is needed between the small businessmen in commerce and the professionals who sell services, the latter are treated as "professional workers." Communication with the community and with others in business is vital for the entrepreneur and for executives of firms. For Negro businessmen there are a number of unique issues. First, Negro business is found almost entirely in the ghetto. Insofar as business is conducted from a fixed facility it is located in an area of concentrated Negro commerce. Few Negroes (none in the research city, to our knowledge) are located in downtown office buildings. When Negro commercial organizations sell to whites, they do so as mobile agents or representatives, or they sell to indigent whites in a Negro community. Negro business is with Negro clients. Second, large Negro businesses are rare and they do not compete directly with whites. With these limitations, Negro business life is much like white business life, except that Negroes lack many of the conditions necessary to success. Formal authority is limited or nonexistent in the small proprietorship. The informal norms of the community, however, may bear greatly on the businessman, and his membership in community businessmen's associations is greatly to his advantage. Many of his important ties with the financial structure of the community are possible only in this way. If we say that unions are not voluntary associations, we might consistently say that businessmen's associations are not voluntary either. There is, however, no categorical exclusion of the proprietor from the right to do business for these reasons alone. The man can stay in business and not belong, but he might have a difficult time of it. It is therefore necessary to distinguish types of voluntary associations to which proprietors belong and types of businesses according to their requirements for social integration.

Professional

The strongest social bonds we will find are among professional workers. In a profession, careful analysis of problems takes place based on theory and accumulation of knowledge. A professional is educated and intensely trained to rationally apply his knowledge. He must also use social relations instrumentally to provide the conditions for successful application of his knowledge. Thorough professionalization includes intentional social relations as a part of the job definition, and the high level of differentiation true of those professions is accompanied by ethically stylized communication based on a specific set of values (often written codes of ethics). Where the worker has legitimized professional standing we would expect, de facto, a high rate of voluntary association membership because professional associations are agencies of legitimation. Where the professional is also an entrepreneur, as is often the case in dentistry, mortuary science, engineering, architecture, law, medicine, and pharmacy, he will have a high rate of membership in business associations as well as professional ones. Theoretically, we would expect the entrepreneurial professional to be the most pluralist of all citizens, that is, to have the highest rate of voluntary association membership. It should be noted again that it is not status that accounts for membership here, but specific occupational pressures. Status may even be partially the consequence rather than the cause of the membership that the work requires.

What are the structural features of the work of a bureaucratic professional? First, the bureaucratic professional usually receives a salary rather than the fees or profits of the entrepreneurial professional, except in notable cases where the professional is able to gain fees in a bureaucratic setting, such as the physician's fee from his hospitalized patient. It is notable that Warner's Index of Status Characteristics scale awards higher ranking to fees and profits than to salary.[23] We cannot presume this to be true among Negroes, although it seems on cursory examination to be an adequate distinction in many professions. One example may serve to illustrate the need for caution here. The Negro lawyer's business consists of an immense number of petit cases in which collection of fees is unremunerative, while his clients may feel compelled to see a white attorney in important cases which require powerful advocacy. Despite the Negro attorney's usefulness to his community, he may be poor and insecure, compared to the salaried teacher. Insofar as status refers to economic affairs, he may be far lower than his occupational identity would indicate (i.e., he experiences status inconsistency vis à vis the white community). Educated Negro professionals are therefore often driven to bureaucratic employment. This drastically shapes the status structure and behavior of the Negro middle class, which is deficient in entrepreneurial professionals as well as in commercial proprietors.

The bureaucratic professional works in an authority setting capable of compelling specific and standardized performance. This performance rests on measured technical competence and is accompanied by recognition of the right of the worker to utilize standards in his work that are oriented to universalistic values. Notable among these sources are professional and educational associations and fraternities. Businesses and public agencies that require high technical competence find it necessary to encourage workers to organize associations that support development of this competence. This kind of association is, however, a source of reinforcement to the employee, particularly since he has privileged access to the facilities and communication channels of the bureaucracy. The professional bureaucratic employee is in a good position to realize the potential power of independent organization and is educated enough to see the relation of his position in the organization to his life in the community. In addition, the bureaucracy frequently has responsibilities in the community that provide structure, germane sources of contact and involvement for the professional.

The number of potential employers for the Negro bureaucratic professional is limited by the size and kind of the organizations that will employ him: there may be only one school system for the teacher, only a few welfare organizations for the social worker, a few law firms for the attorney, a few major firms for the engineer, and so on. Professional voluntary associations in turn find that national organizations are a necessity to set standards and to provide mobility opportunities or a source of countervailing power to the monolithic employer. Bureaucratic professionals may thus become cosmopolitan rather than local, or more oriented to the profession than the community. By contrast, the employee of a national firm, often a nonprofessional, is oriented to the company more than the profession and again may be only casually interested in the community. If we disregard the professional voluntary associations, which are joined by typical bureaucratic professionals such as teachers, welfare workers, and engineers, their membership rates in the remaining voluntary associations may not be any higher than is indicated by their collegiality and coracialism.

When we encounter such plural normative sources we will use the term *emploity*, a term parallel to *polity* in politics. This indicates that institutionalization of control mechanisms concerning work and workers is integrated with the normative structure of plural organizations or groups. Such a concept is needed in order to counteract the mislead-

ing assumption, typical of most studies of work, that a person
is responsive only to the organization that pays him. Theoretically, the emploity may operate for both entrepreneurial and
bureaucratic professionals, as well as for any worker to some
extent—it is introduced here because of its salience for bureaucratic professionals. The emploity is characterized by potential transfer of the association-determining operation of
employment to more abstract levels or to superordinate or
separated community forms. When we do research on the
voluntary associations of professionals, therefore, we must not
lose sight of the meaning of the unit "voluntary association."
The successful physician, for example, may be on a number of
regional or national committees that give him much power
and prestige but in effect take him out of contact with local
organizations. In a similar way, the occupational community
of the union member limits his social relations and voluntary
association memberships to specific collectivities which are
structurally separated from the residential community.

For the Negro professional the community offers limited
employment choices, and therefore he faces obstacles to the
development of his power unless he opts to move to another
community and begin again. On the other hand, blue-collar
workers, whether Negro or white, may find a great many
similar places of work nearby, and can possibly escape from
the authority of any particular employer.

In sum, we can conclude that the voluntary association
memberships of the Negro bureaucratic professional are highly
channeled as the consequence of a unique kind of accommodation between authority and reinforcement. In addition,
coracialism and collegiality are also high. We will find in
this case, then, that both the number and the kind of voluntary associations belonged to are predictable.

The Negro entrepreneurial professional, on the other hand, faces a completely different situation, for his customers take the place of an employer, and they do not exert a structured authority over his behavior. He can, in fact, selectively ignore or mistreat some of them for a considerable period of time before he suffers any loss of business, as long as his occupation is in particular demand in his area. In the long run, the market more than the emploity itself exerts powerful norms over his behavior, coupled with the extensive socialization to values that is carried out in professional training. The individual is autonomous in his local sphere and is likely to be active in a number of community affairs, maximizing opportunities to control the community on behalf of his business or his personal values. The Negro entrepreneurial professional operates almost entirely in the Negro community and therefore lacks coracialism because he has few employees or partners. Customers or clients may become an indirect source of coracialism for him, in his continual involvement with them in the ghetto. This interesting case cannot be adequately studied in our work because there are actually so few entrepreneurial professionals in the Negro community (a fact that has often been bemoaned by those who wish to see improvement in the lot of Negroes).

THE STRUCTURE OF WORK AND VOLUNTARY ASSOCIATION MEMBERSHIP

We promised to examine the effects of coracialism, reinforcement, and collegiality with a view to understanding their consequences for membership in voluntary associations. In this consideration of the social relations at work, it has been seen that certain additional conditions affect the worker's participation. These include several that have the effect of limiting the participation or membership of the worker or of affecting the kind of association to which he will be oriented. The particular set of factors we will consider next has to do with the unintended consequences of the structural features of hiring, scheduling of work, and the physical setting of the job. These structural features have the consequence of setting in motion processes which, secondarily, guide the workers' participation.

Let us change stance here and examine these character-istics without systematically attempting to characterize each occupational status.

One such process involves social relationships created to assure hiring suitable workers for jobs that are sporadic or that involve frequent crew changes or schedule variations. Where work requires a high level of skill, and where skills must be coordinated, a source of social relationships is gen-erated. In these jobs, one qualification is the ability to com-municate. Where work also specifies that the application of skill take place in an event, like a musical performance, or in a delimited period of time, and where errors are costly, it becomes necessary for the employer to consider the values of the individual who is hired, insofar as these values are related to problems of working with others. Where perform-ance must be guaranteed, norms become more imperative. This often occurs in the building trades and particularly concerns those with traditional skills such as carpentry, paint-ing, and the like. Musicians and certain entertainers are organizationally similar even though the skills appear to be vastly different. This is another instance of common types of social organization occurring across the typical boundary lines of the blue-collar and white-collar work.

In cases where hiring is repeatedly done by a foreman or an individual who may contract for a small job, it becomes necessary for such a person to have an inventory of workers with specific skills and abilities of communication. By contrast, the union hiring hall tends to develop a type of selection based on rational rules, albeit altered on occasion by favoritism.[24] In Tampa, only one major hiring hall involves any considerable number of Negroes, that of the Longshoremen's Union. It is controlled by Negro officers and members.

Less strong relations occur when direct hiring is done by employers who have functionaries to select employees from a list of the formally qualified. Civil service systems that operate on this basis may alienate workers even though they separate the functions of work from examination, selection, and hiring. Yet they do offer a formal source of reinforcement for the worker's claims to rights. Programs of the United States Office of Economic Opportunity, in their early phases at the time of field work (1967), present a mixed picture, in which the individual (either Negro or white) is given considerable reinforcement as well as training but is not typically or necessarily placed in a situation in which social relationships develop at work.

Where hiring is done by a foreman or subcontractor there is a tendency for groups to form among workers. This is because such employers have a preferred list of workers whom they know to be mutually compatible or who are acceptable to important others. One study in a northern setting showed that building trades organized in this way often had work crews with an ethnic identity. Comparably, many unions articulate along racial lines.[25]

What are the consequences of these arrangements of hiring and scheduling? Although there is no direct research on the matter, materials relating to the study of occupational communities provide a provisional formulation for answers.

When hiring practices or the work situation are organized so that association between workers off the job is normal and workers interact off the job with consciousness of their work identities, cohesive groups may result. Where this is pervasive, stable, and enduring, we find an "occupational community."[26] For example, Lipset, Trow, and Coleman found that members of the International Typographers' Union (who formed an occupational community) frequently contacted one another off the work scene, formed clubs and interest groups, and were very active in union affairs. On the other hand, Blum found that meat-packers (supra, the category of normative independent task workers or mass production workers) rarely contacted one another off the job.[27] W. F. Cottrell's study of railroad workers revealed that their participation in community affairs was drastically limited by the time structure of their occupation, but social relations with other railroaders were made possible.[28] Formation of an occupational community by Negroes is theoretically possible, but the conditions of strong unionism under which known instances occur are rarely found among Negroes in southern cities.

A community typically is conceived in sociology as a comprehensive social relationship that may take place in a number of different ways, or even be absent, in the urban setting. The occupational community is a form of community articulated about a particular employit which, because of its configuration, has the ability to organize the lives of its members in a comprehensive way.

Perhaps a caution is advisable at this point. It is tempting to overgeneralize about occupational communities and assume that they have beneficial consequences for societies by providing continuity, wholeness, stability, and other good things. This is the stuff of which introductory sociology text ideologies are made. We make no judgments about the meaning of communities, nor of occupational communities. We merely wish to show that where a condition exists that we call "occupational community," following Lipset et al., it is the consequence of a certain ordering of the structure of work. The important issue for our analysis is that the occupational community typically (but not necessarily) is associated with a decrease in the voluntary associational life of the residential community (independent of the possible increase in voluntary associational life of members of the occupational community) because, as Cottrell pointed out in his classic study, work rules the life of the worker so that all other schedules and relations must be sacrificed, with the consequence that the railroader cannot participate in regular meetings and activities. Lipset et al. advance the thesis that the well-known democracy of the International Typographers' Union is due to the occupational community with its associated internal social relations and voluntary associations. They do not make the claim that these conditions contribute to workers' democratic participation in the residential community. We would carry the analysis further and point out that the occupational community contributes to the workers' integration only with workers of his union and shop, and he is integrated with society as a whole only if the union and

the shop as units are integrated into society in some meaningful way.[29] The member of an occupational community
may be numbered with the mass rather than the pluralist
society. The occupational community is then an intervening
structure between work and society, which is generated by
the structure of hiring and scheduling. In our field research we
asked only what the person belonged to, not whether the
organization was integrated with society, and thus we must be
content with indirect evidence for the views advanced here.

Germane to the problem of hiring are other aspects of
work that have effects similar to those of occupational communities but that do not necessarily have the community-
forming qualities mentioned above. When work is organized
under strong authority into time units such that completion
of a work sequence is imperative regardless of its situation
in time or space, we will speak of *work imperialism.*

The typical community has diurnal phasing, with its
rhythm of daytime routines integrated about men's work, children's and women's activities, and nighttime routines of
family, community meetings, and leisure. The mismatching
of cycles or rhythms of those who work while the community
does not may be termed *phase segregation.* Phase segregation
is a regular or systematic disjunction of persons and communities; work imperialism typically produces an erratic and
unpredictable disjunction. Both, however, are differently experienced by race and class, which is the main issue here.

A brief example is perhaps in order before returning to
theoretical issues. In the early days of the development of antipoverty programs in Tampa there was a considerable conflict over the time of committee meetings. White community
leaders consistently exerted their influence to hold meetings

in the daytime, when minorities could not attend. Generally, the whites were sufficiently high in the occupational world that they could control their own allocation of time, while nonwhites and the poor were subject to work imperialism. If it became necessary to meet in the daytime, night-shift workers sometimes had to interrupt their afternoon rest to attend. We would hazard the guess that if the voluntary associations that the lower classes cannot attend due to phase segregation and work imperialism were added to their membership scores, and the meetings that the middle classes attend because their careers depended on it were subtracted, the difference in voluntary association participation between the two due to social class characteristics alone would be much smaller than they now appear.

Phase segregation and work imperialism are accompanied by adaptive responses of those employees who accept them as a condition of work. Typically, they are accepted because other things make it possible or necessary (i.e., there are associated rewards or losses). Among the typical adaptations to or consequences of phase segregation are: irregular family life, perhaps associated with familial role abdication; limitation of involvement in those voluntary associations that require regular participation (in religious organizations, participation might be in the church rather than the less permissive sect); and acceptance of leisure patterns that rely on ubiquitous media such as hobbies or television rather than neighborhood voluntary associations. Although residential community life suffers, the consequence may be occupational communities (if other conditions of the ordering of work are also present). In passing, it should be pointed out that some of the social participation found by Lipset, Trow, and Cole-

man among the typographers happened because typographers
were thrown together by work imperialism and phase segregation and not because of the conditions of the place of work
or of the union itself.

Occupations typical of Negroes that involve phase segregation include railroading, industrial plant shift work, and
cab-driving. Work imperialism is a major factor that occurs
in commercial entertaining, trucking, harvesting, packing
perishable goods, crisis control or service work, demeaning
work subject to man's whim or petulance. The list could be
extended but the examples are already too long. If we add
the aspect of spatial segregation, we have generalized the
most important features of time and space that control social
relations.

Let us specify certain occupations typically performed by
Negroes in Tampa in which phase segregation or work imperialism occur. Longshoremen work until the job is completed, which may be several days, followed by equivalent
time off. Pullman porters work by the trip. Caterers work
according to the demand created by holidays, special events,
and celebrations. Shrimp-packers may work long hours when
the boats come in. Fruit pickers and packers have long periods
of work interrupted by unpredictable slack time due to
weather and equipment failure. Roadside pickup workers
wait by the highway in two areas in the city for casual employers in order to do unskilled, manual work for irregular
periods.

This attention to work imperialism and phase segregation employment of blue-collar workers does not imply that
white-collar workers are not subjected to it. Among entrepreneurial professionals, the undertaker works when he has

raw materials, and the obstetrician puts in overtime in emergencies. But those who bring expert technical service to the lives of others typically have compensating arrangements.

And, if we mention blue-collar and white-collar workers, we must not forget those who wear no shirts at all. The prostitute works when work is to be done, and she rarely gets a chance to attend the regular meetings of the Women's Club or the PTA. There are a large number of minority personnel in occupations geared to others' indulgence, binges, or immoralities, and they typically work the shift following the work of others.

While phase segregation and work imperialism operate to lessen the opportunity to participate in the routines of voluntary associations, it must not be assumed that this necessarily means a decrease in membership. For example, Pullman porters are subject to work imperialism but the historic commitment of their union to civil rights results in frequent membership in the NAACP, although perhaps infrequent attendance at meetings. Many voluntary associations are adapted to high membership but low participation. We would expect workers who encounter phase segregation and work imperialism to find such high-membership, low-participation groups satisfactory vehicles for symbolic affiliation with instrumental associations, although they would be inappropriate for expressive voluntary associations, which are oriented to participation as a means of gratification. Conversely, we would expect expressive voluntary associations to have high ratios of participation to membership, and instrumental associations to have lower ratios, except in their founding or social-movement phases where participation is equivalent with membership.

Now we have completed consideration of the probable

pluralistic consequences of the several occupational status levels of the work that Negroes do and we have analyzed the importance of hiring and scheduling. Ideally, research to test these ideas on the relation of work and voluntary association membership would begin at the place of work, with each type of work represented in appropriate samples and with all of the kinds of relationships traced in detail. Theoretically desirable as this may be, it is too difficult in practice. Merely to find the places and types of work and sample them adequately would presuppose a survey comparable to the one that is the final source for our research here. It became apparent early in our research planning that research must be confined to a sample of workers in the community, and not of places of work. The theory we shall test will then be centered on the worker. It may be stated thus: *The amount and kind of participation of Negroes in voluntary associations can be predicted from knowledge of their formal and informal social relations at work and from community and personal factors related to them.*

HYPOTHESES

To facilitate easy consideration of the relationship of theory to hypotheses, the hypotheses will be listed here, and discussion of their derivation and application will follow.

Hypothesis 1. The greater the coracialism, the greater the total voluntary association membership.

Hypothesis 2. The greater the reinforcement, the more likely the Negro will participate in Negro-rights organizations.

Hypothesis 3. Collegiality strengthens the effect of other variables related to voluntary association membership, but is not the sole reason for membership.

In the discussion leading to formulation of the theory we examined a number of situations in which the structure of work either made possible or inhibited the operation of the social relations that cause membership. We proposed concepts to cover the most frequently encountered types. These concepts include phase segregation, work imperialism, emploity, and authority. These in turn are interrelated. To formulate hypotheses concerning the effect of each set would create a bewildering network of hypotheses. Instead, we will select for presentation here only a few to illustrate the dynamics of social relations and the structure of work in predicting voluntary association membership.

Coracialism and collegiality are concepts referring to two kinds of informal relationships, which may be interrelated in complex ways. The former refers to the availability of Negro companionship on the job and, of course, it cannot exist if there are no coworkers. Conversely, collegiality represents the extent of friendship (regardless of race) on the job, and may exist only if there are people to fill the requirements. Typically, when coracialism is present it becomes collegiality, but this is not necessary, and so we asked the respondent about both. Again, when collegiality is present it may or may not lead to solidarity based on race, either by definition (no Negroes present) or because Negroes' friendship choices do not, for a variety of reasons, include other Negroes, or because of ecological factors. Hypothesis 1, which states that coracialism leads to voluntary association membership, starts from the assumption that in a segregated and discriminatory society, racial solidarity occurs under conditions

of reference-race availability. This is something more than
an assumption, however, since in a preliminary study we found
that the expected positive relationship between coracialism
(called *support* in that study) and NAACP membership was
present.[30] One consequence, then, of racial solidarity at work
is a greater likelihood of membership in some types of voluntary associations.

Reinforcement is an extrasystemic force (or outside force
or power) that intervenes in the operations of an economic
enterprise. Of the many such forces operating in this way,
we have selected only two: the union and civil service. At a
later point we will examine the operation of the professional
voluntary association, which exerts an influence that is similar
in many ways.

Reinforcement has complex direct and indirect effects
on voluntary association membership. The Negro may encounter discrimination on the job or attempts at interference
with his rights as a person or as a citizen, and in such cases
he will be more able to gain justice if he has access to help
from outside sources. One such issue has to do with the right
to participate in controversial or militant Negro-rights organizations, if he so chooses. At least two major all-Negro unions
in Tampa have a reputation for direct aid to Negro causes.
A second consequence of reinforcement is that it typically involves protection against arbitrary or systematic actions of
employers regarding worker security, seniority, layoff, wage
changes, and other such grievances. Workers who enjoy the
backing afforded by reinforcement probably have greater
continuity of employment and generally improved security,
which results in their ability to plan ahead, buy property,
and in many ways to find good reason to join the full life

of the community. By use of one concept, we obscure some of these grievances and we can expect our research to reveal some irregular results when reinforcement is used alone. Therefore, we will typically take a second step and analyze variations in the results along lines indicated by the presence or absence of our other variables.

The fact that a Negro is helped by an outside force does not of itself indicate that he will belong to a voluntary association. It says only that he is in a better position to participate in community life. Hypothesis 2, it may be recalled, had to do with the tendency to join Negro-rights organizations. To understand this, we must consider the nature of the organizations that come to the aid of the Negro as a Negro. The unions to which Negroes belong are often Negro unions in a Negro community. Civil service is often in the hands of whites. We therefore would expect in the case of the unions that the effect of reinforcement would be polarized about the issue of race itself. In contrast, the security-conferring effectiveness of Negro unions will be found to be relatively weaker than that of white unions. Union membership for a Negro in a Negro union means racial solidarity, and the effect is like that of coracialism, except that it has the further result of involving him in an organization that speaks for Negroes, emphasizes Negro rights, and tends to make common cause with other organizations working for the same ends in the community at large. Moreover, the solidarity derived from reinforcement extends beyond the place of work, although it is still occupationally generated.

Since a union is an association (although rarely a completely voluntary one) participation in it might produce a tendency to participate in voluntary associations due to role learning, socialization to values regarding participation, and so on.

This may also be true concerning the part played by the church in facilitating community participation. Joining and participating in esteemed organizations brings certain consequences typically favorable to joining others, as we noted earlier concerning unions. These consequences include role learning, personal satisfaction, and friendship.[31] Because the church is ubiquitous in the Negro community, we will give it close attention as a channel to first acquaintance with community organizations. In addition, the satellite organizations of the church and those semisecular clubs and societies observed in Negro churches in Tampa are significant as frequent sources of entry into voluntary community associations. Since our theory concerns work and not community organizations as independent variables, we cannot use it to deduce the effect of church membership on voluntary associations. It would, however, strengthen our argument about the part played by the union and other community associations to verify the part played by church membership. We will, therefore, attempt to verify the collateral hypothesis (the term will be used throughout) that those who belong to a church more often belong to one or more voluntary associations, and that those who belong to church-related organizations will more often belong to one or more additional voluntary associations.

THE RESEARCH

At the beginning of this chapter, we pointed out that our sources of information included observation of and participation in the research area, and three formal studies. The last of these field studies presented the opportunity for testing the hypotheses developed in this chapter. We now turn to a brief description of the methods of research in the last study.

Trained Negro interviewers conducted 1,086 interviews of Negroes in Tampa, Florida in 1967. A two-stage sample was used, with special care taken to include isolated Negro families in fringe areas. Dwelling units were pre-enumerated. A seventy-item schedule (see Appendix A) was administered in the home. Interviews were confined to people between twenty and sixty years of age. Up to eight attempts were made to contact the predesignated individual. If no one worked, or if more than one person worked, the head of the household was interviewed; if only one person within the age limits worked he was selected regardless of his or her status in the household. The final sample consisted of 727 males and 359 females. Seven of the males and 37 of the females were not the head of the house. Of those interviewed who were not working, 35 were the male head of house, 94 were the female head of house, and 11 were females who were not the head of house. Other characteristics of the sample are presented in the later chapters. Appendix B lists other characteristics of the sample.

The significance of this sampling method can be better understood if we consider the other ways that sampling might have been done. As previously mentioned, the most obvious would be the method of contacting Negroes on the job and interviewing them there. The chances for error are great, however, since it is almost impossible in this way to get an adequate sample of work places or privacy to ask about controversial issues. Since Negroes very often work for small enterprises, the difficulty of locating them is even greater. We chose to contact people in their homes to assure an adequate sample of workers regardless of where they worked.

The twenty to sixty age limits were chosen since the very old have low rates of voluntary association membership. A bias is thereby introduced and our net membership may appear to be somewhat higher than the typical sample of all adults. In a similar sense, selection of the head of the household has a biasing effect which produces a slightly higher rate of membership.

Of special interest was the Tampa riot of June 11, 1967, which happened when interviewing was about three-quarters completed. Numerous pre- and postriot comparisons of data were subsequently made and where the riot appeared to have an effect on the data an explanation is introduced. The riot also made possible the analysis of the relation of work, riot, and voluntary association which appears as a separate chapter.

Theoretical concepts must be given practical form under local conditions. To this end, the concepts were operationalized as follows. A coracialism index was developed to combine information concerning the race of the person having authority over the respondent, and the race of the respondent's fellow workers. If the respondent had a Negro supervisor he was classified as having high coracialism. If the person in immediate authority was a white, the race of his fellow workers was considered: if he had Negro or both Negro and white fellow workers, he was classified as having medium coracialism. If he had only white fellow workers or worked alone, the respondent with a white supervisor was classified as having low coracialism. The classification is not logically exhaustive, but it covers all situations that were found. It must be remembered that the data consists of the respondents' statements about these matters, which was probably an issue only in the case of the "race of fellow workers" question. Thus, if the respondent said that he worked alone, he was placed in a low coracialism category. It may be that his statement that he works alone reflects the immediate nature of his work rather than the overall situation in his place of work. A truckdriver may say that he works alone but the firm may employ many Negro truckdrivers with whom he has an opportunity to associate at some time during the work day. Thus, low coracialism respondents will include those who would better be placed, given our objective, in the medium category. Still, we accepted the subjective statement of the individual.

Reinforcement consists of having union or civil-service status. More detailed and less decisive aspects had to be ignored, since testing for them involved detail that would excessively lengthen the interviews. Therefore we expect that the hypothesis tested using this measure will not always be as clear-cut as desired. An index that combined coracialism and reinforcement was designed to investigate the possibility of joint effects. The combined index was thus expanded to a six-point scale in which at each coracialism level those with civil service or union membership were differentiated from those without such membership.

The third index was of collegiality. This index represents the extent to which the respondent interacted (presumably informally) with some of the workers on the job and the extent to which his friends in the community worked with him. For respondents who had neither friends as fellow workers nor interaction with fellow workers on the job, a further distinction was made between those who said they worked alone and those who said they worked with others. The remainder of the responses were scaled so that the top collegiality position consisted of respondents with at least some of their "close friends" as job colleagues, who also said that when away from work they "talked a lot" to their fellow workers.

The questionnaire is reproduced in Appendix A. It features methods in which common language categories are used to sensitize the respondent, and actual responses are written down. Successive inquiries obtain the name of the voluntary association, and the respondents' attendance and office holding.

NOTES

1. Some of the more famous studies of communities in American sociology may be cited by way of illustration, including St. Clair Drake and Horace R. Cayton, *Black Metropolis;* August B. Hollingshead, *Elmtown's Youth;* Robert S. Lynd and Helen M. Lynd, *Middletown;* and *Middletown in Transition;* W. Lloyd Warner and Paul S. Lunt, *The Social Life of a Modern Community.* Many less well-known works are of the same kind, dating back many years. The following, arranged in rough chronological sequence, all touch on voluntary associations without arriving at what we could consider to be theoretical generalizations of consequence: Albert Blumenthal, *Small Town Stuff;* Edward R. Roper Power, "The Social Structure of an English County Town," *Sociological Review* 29: 391–413; Terence Young, *Beacontree and Dagenham;* Ruth Durant, *Watling;* M. Penelope Hall, *Community Centers and Associations in Manchester;*

Thomas Cauter and John S. Downham, *The Communication of Ideas.* Other significant studies might be cited, but a complete list will not be attempted here.

2. "In no country in the world has the principle of association been more successfully used, or applied to a greater multitude of objects, than in America" (Alexis de Tocqueville, *Democracy in America,* p. 95). Actually, if we compare the voluntary aspects of the American church organization to European churches, the matter goes back much further. For a good sample of thought on the church as a voluntary association, see D. B. Robertson, ed., *Voluntary Associations, A Study of Groups in Free Societies: Essays in Honor of James Luther Adams.*

3. In recent work of Booth, voluntary associations are analyzed as the consequence of social contacts, and the analysis thus does not depend on status assumptions. Alan J. Booth, "Personal Influence and the Decision to Participate in Voluntary Associations" (Paper presented at the 1966 Meeting of the American Sociological Association). A somewhat similar treatment is found in the work of Babchuk. Nicholas Babchuk and C. Wayne Gordon, *The Voluntary Association in the Slum.*

4. Eugene Litwak, "Voluntary Associations and Neighborhood Cohesion." Similar findings are reported by Peter Rossi, "Voluntary Associations in an Industrial City." Pellegrin and Coates examine the place of social relations among executives and the community. Roland J. Pellegrin and Charles H. Coates, "Absentee-Owned Corporations and Community Power Structure," *American Journal of Sociology* 61: 413–419.

5. Aileen Ross, "Philanthropic Activity in the Business Career," in *Man, Work and Society,* ed. Sigmund Nosow and William H. Form.

6. William Spinrad, "Correlates of Trade Union Participation," *American Sociological Review* 25:237–244.

7. The work of Babchuk and Gordon, *The Voluntary Association in the Slum,* is perhaps the most comprehensive empirical study of voluntary associations in Negro and in contrasting white life, and is of particular value because it is concerned

with lower-class life in an urban area. It does not, however, take
up the consequences of this contrast. Moreover, the relation of
work and membership is not specific. If we pursue our topic as
an independent variable, the results are equally disappointing.
The employment of Negroes is a major national goal at the time
of writing, but none of the numerous works on the issue are
germane. The voluminous anthology, *Negroes and Jobs,* does
not even index voluntary associations. Louis A. Ferman, Joyce L.
Kornbluh, and J. A. Miller, eds., *Negroes and Jobs: A Book of
Readings.*

8. Arnold M. Rose, *Theory and Method in the Social
Sciences,* p. 30. The theory is developed more comprehensively
in Arnold M. Rose, *The Power Structure.*

9. William Kornhauser, *The Politics of Mass Society,* p. 39.

10. National Advisory Commission on Civil Disorders, *Report of the National Advisory Commission on Civil Disorders.*

11. This is true of Florida cities in general.

12. Kornhauser, *Politics of Mass Society,* p. 41. The other
two possible combinations of accessibility and elitism result in
"communal" and "totalitarian" societies, which are not relevant
to this discusion. Of special interest are two unique polar cases
of relation of work and community in which work organizes the
community and the reverse: the planned and integrated intentional community (e.g., the kibbutz), which is the consequence
of an associational community controlling work; and the "occupational community," in which a comprehensive form of integrated social life emerges from the associational relations of
workers in a plant or shop controlled by a strong union. Neither
of these involves voluntary associations directly, although formal
organization is involved at some point in the parent structure.
This analysis might be extended to a variety of other forms, including the "organization man" of Whyte's analysis. William H.
Whyte, Jr., *The Organization Man.*

13. Breed points out that pluralism is not a characteristic
of the southern United States. Warren Breed, "Group Structure
and Resistance to Desegregation in the Deep South," *Social*

Problems 10: 84–94. Gary Marx found that voluntary association membership was positively related to militancy. Gary Marx, *Protest and Prejudice,* p. 7. It would seem to follow that mass society is not militant. We shall return to this point when we examine specific types of organizations to which Negroes belong.

14. Rose subscribes to such a view of the "Power Structure" in relationship to voluntary associations. See Arnold M. Rose, *The Power Structure.*

15. Unlike the other three concepts defined here, authority will be used without operational specification or numerical scores. It is present, or not, as a phenomenon of organizational type, as the thing that gives meaning to the others. Self-employed or person-employed workers experience "legitimated ability" indirectly, mediated through less direct mechanisms, and we will not call this influence "authority." This is one important reason for introducing distinctions, at a later point, about the type of employment. Here authority is a general term, used to develop a general theory about the other variables, but it will be seen to be strictly applicable only to our cases of larger formal organizations, which we call "company-employed."

16. David Matza, "Poverty and Disrepute," in *Contemporary Social Problems,* 2d ed., ed. Robert K. Merton and Robert A. Nisbet, p. 628.

17. Drake and Cayton, *Black Metropolis,* 2:524.

18. Thus, in most survey research, the underworld and the overworld are underrepresented, which should point to a moral of some kind. There is a sociological implication: both precision and specification of possible error in sampling are vital, and we shall return to this where appropriate.

19. Domestic work is undergoing change, particularly in regard to Negroes. The proportion of whites in domestic work is rising in the South, and attempts are being made to upgrade the work itself into a kind of home-service profession. Some of the issues are dealt with by David Chaplin, "Domestic Service and the Negro," in *Blue-Collar World: Studies of the American Worker,* ed. Arthur B. Shostak and William Gomberg. A back-

ground study on the domestic worker was prepared for this research, comparing Tampa and Boston, Florida and Massachusetts, using census data for these units. See Jack C. Ross, "301–887: Doing Whitey's Dirty Work," mimeographed.

20. Hylan Lewis showed that Negro domestics in a small Piedmont town frequently had high status among Negroes due to their access to news, their regularity of work, and the status of the family with whom the work was done. This small town had had a highly compressed Negro status structure, which does not apply to a large urban setting. Hylan Lewis, *Blackways of Kent,* chap. 10. Today full-time domestic work is being replaced in large southern cities by "day's work," which is an occupation that Negro women can easily enter and easily leave, and is thus adapted to the marriage career. The suburban, white, middle-class housewife sees the Negro domestic as a rather cheap laborer to do the unpleasant tasks that remain after she has used all of the automatic household machines her husband's credit rating will allow. The importance of day's work may be easily underestimated by the casual observer. In one census tract in Tampa, at any one time as many as one-third of the nonwhite (mostly Negro) women in the labor force are domestics. A much higher fraction may do day's work at some time in their lives, and thus the social relationships established in such contacts may have a far-reaching effect on the attitudes of both Negroes and whites toward each other, as well as a normative effect during the period of employment.

21. During the study, we had the opportunity to observe Negro and white labor groups of this type. An ideal observation station was available: a new social science building was being erected close to the authors' office windows and for a year we (among other things) watched construction workers without being observed. Some conclusions: in any task situation, Negroes usually work more, do the heavier and the dirtier part. Whites loaf more, and more confidently. Negroes are frequently idle, but look ready to work. Upon examination, much of the Negro workers' idleness seems to stem from the racial differen-

tiation of tasks. For example, the Negro is not allowed to be a mason but he may stand virtually idle for hours and occasionally hand the bricks to a white who will set the work pace. Racial differentiation of tasks exacerbated by work rules is inflexible and not easily adapted to efficient division of labor and use of time. A "hurry up and wait" condition results, wherein Negroes on the same job as whites are erratically overworked and bored, and, withall, alienated from their work. The plight of the Army private, who is also in a caste social structure, is similar. The basic sociological issue is the combination of a normative division of labor under union (or traditional) work rules (such as in the building trades) and the existence of comprehensive segregation as a normative value in the community. Thus the practical consequences of a normative division of labor depend on the community context.

22. C. Wright Mills identified the work characteristics of white-collar production workers (C. Wright Mills, *White Collar*). He did not, however, treat the issue of the Negro white-collar worker. Many Negroes work in small firms and have many tasks that require some paper work, but not enough to become an office specialty. In the Old South the solution typically was to use Negroes to do the manual and whites to do the writing parts, no matter how inefficient that might become. When we encounter Negroes as white-collar production workers, it is frequently in larger national firms with fair employment commitments, which are sources of reinforcement. One of the reasons there are so few Negro clerks in the South is the Negroes' lack of education, but more important is the lack of large businesses (now changing) that employ Negroes, and in which it is structurally feasible to have full-time specialists at mental tasks. As long as Negro businesses are small and large businesses discriminate, there will be few Negro clerical workers, and a major source of mobility to middle-class status remains severed.

23. W. Lloyd Warner, Marchia Meeker, and Kenneth Eells, *Social Status in America: A Manual of Procedure for the Measurement of Social Status,* p. 123.

24. Greer treats the operation of the hiring hall in detail, particularly regarding favoritism and racial bias. Scott Greer, *Last Man In.*

25. Richard R. Myers, "Interpersonal Relations in the Building Industry," in *Man, Work and Society,* ed. Sigmund Nosow and William H. Form. Warner and Low show how ethnic identity is intimately involved in hiring and promotion in a New England factory. W. Lloyd Warner and J. O. Low, *The Social System of the Modern Factory.* Collins' work examines similar issues. See Orvis Collins, "Ethnic Behavior in Industry: Sponsorship and Rejection in a New England Factory," *American Journal of Sociology* 51: 293–298. Dewey distinguishes jobs of short duration, in which Negro and white are employed to work side by side, from longer term work in which a racial division of labor assumes stable form. Donald Dewey, "Negro Employment in Southern Industry," *Journal of Political Economy* 60: 279–293. Everett Hughes has dealt with discrimination in industry in a number of works, but deals only tangentially with the issues examined here.

26. The concept is found in Seymour M. Lipset, Martin Trow, and J. S. Coleman, *Union Democracy,* p. x.

27. Fred Blum, *Toward a Democratic Work Process.*

28. W. F. Cottrell, "Of Time and the Railroader," *American Sociological Review* 4: 190–198; and idem, *The Railroader.*

29. Similar conclusions were reached by Reitzes in his study of racial attitudes in unions. He found that the members of a union supported racial integration in unions, but in their own neighborhood they opposed housing integration. The illustration is especially apt because no claim is made by Reitzes that the union had a high rate of solidarity due to occupational community development among its members. Members were responsive, instead, to a discriminatory property owners' association in the neighborhood in which they lived. Dietrich C. Reitzes, "Union vs. Neighborhood in a Tension Situation," in *Racial and Ethnic Relations,* ed. Bernard L. Segal.

30. Jack C. Ross and Raymond Wheeler, "Structural Sources

of Threat to Negro Membership in Militant Voluntary Associations in a Southern City," *Social Forces* 45: 583–586. This is the study based on a sample of 256 cases that was referred to at the beginning of this chapter.

31. Numerous studies support the idea that personal contacts are favorable to joining, among which are the studies already cited by Booth, "Personal Influence and the Decision to Participate," and Babchuk and Gordon, *The Voluntary Association in the Slum.* Supporting evidence was found by David L. Sills, *The Volunteers: Means and Ends in a National Organization.* Our point is that belonging to a first organization becomes the basis for potential membership in a second, limited, of course, by many factors. The reason for including the church in our study then becomes significant: in the church, childhood socialization to associational life occurs and channels to many forms of community voluntary associational life are established, limited by religious and other evaluations of such contacts.

2

SOURCES
OF
BELONGING

In chapter 1 we considered the theoretical relationships between the work that Negroes do and their membership in voluntary associations. In this chapter we will begin to test the theory by examining the relationship of the independent variables of the three hypotheses with a single dependent variable, total voluntary association memberships. In chapters 3, 4, and 5 we will examine this dependent variable in detail, by considering the variations in the types of voluntary associations to which Negroes belong. Thus, the analysis in this chapter is somewhat provisional, because we will consider the dependent variable to be a unitary phenomenon, when in fact it is not. Chapters 2–5 will be considered a unit, comprising a composite picture of the relationship of coracialism, reinforcement, and collegiality (and the conditions under which they occur) with the amount and kind of membership in community voluntary associations. Before pursuing these issues, we present some general information on the voluntary association memberships of the respondents in our sample.

GENERAL MEMBERSHIP PATTERNS

More than two in five (44 percent) of all respondents belonged to one or more voluntary associations. Although about 41 percent of the males belonged, 49 percent of the females were members. Since sampling priority was given to heads of households, the housewives, other members of households, and older respondents are rarely found in our sample. It is difficult to assess the total effect of sampling criteria on the membership rates, since the criteria did not include those under twenty years of age (who have fewer memberships), but did include females, some of whom have more memberships.

About one-fifth of the respondents have just one voluntary association membership, one-ninth have two memberships, and one tenth have three or more. A few persons have more than ten memberships.

Considerable ambiguity is encountered when we attempt to compare our results with those of other studies, because the major works on membership rates of Negroes are based on national samples, which vary as to inclusion of urban and rural residents. Three studies cited in a study by Hausknecht reveal Negro membership rates that illustrate this point.[1] One of these studies (American Institute of Public Opinion, 1954) found 54 percent; a second (National Opinion Research Center, 1955), 27 percent; and a third (Survey Research Center, 1952) found 69 percent who belonged to at least one voluntary association. Babchuk and Thompson[2] report a Negro membership rate of 75 percent, Wright and Hyman[3] (NORC Survey no. 335) report 25 percent. The Babchuk and Thompson sample might be expected to show a higher rate due to its urban setting (Lincoln, Nebraska) and probably a higher educational level than a national sample would show. Our findings are midway among the percentages of these samples.

It was stated in chapter 1 that churches and unions would not be considered to be voluntary associations, since membership in them typically is either ascriptive or involuntary. They do, however, comprise important parts of the community, and hence we will find occasion to compare them with voluntary associations. We note here simply that almost three-quarters of all respondents claimed church membership, while 15 percent belonged to a union. A more detailed study of churches and unions is presented in chapter 6.

OCCUPATION, SELECTED ATTRIBUTES, AND MEMBERSHIP RATES

Without exception, sociological research has found a positive relationship between higher status and membership in voluntary associations.[4] This is the case for Negroes as well as whites. Our results are no exception: the percentage of respondents with voluntary association memberships is highest for those with the highest status and decreases regularly with decreasing occupational status. (The ranking system follows the order used in chapter 1, reading from low to high status: unskilled; semiskilled and operatives; skilled and craftsmen; clerical and sales; managers, proprietors, and officials; professionals, technical and kindred.) Put in another way, about two-thirds of the respondents with high-status occupations belong to at least one voluntary association, while about two-thirds of the unemployed (mostly unskilled when employed) do not belong at all. Moreover, the category of respondents with five or more memberships consists almost entirely of professionals, plus a few managers. As we move down in status from the professional and technical, we find that the proportion with multiple memberships falls off rapidly in successive categories. We may conclude that the higher the status of the respondent's occupation, the greater the number of voluntary associations to which he belongs.[5] The data is presented in Table 1.

The membership characteristics of the unskilled workers and the unemployed are quite similar, and probably for good reason. Typically working for wages rather than salary, and perhaps working infrequently, the unskilled worker faces financial insecurity and, of special interest to us, employment in work situations conducive to isolation and alienation. To be unemployed and on relief in Florida in 1967 meant receiving a maximum of $84 a month (regardless of family size), which is somewhat less than one-third of what many authorities consider the poverty level for a family of four.

TABLE 1

PERCENTAGE DISTRIBUTION OF VOLUNTARY ASSOCIATION MEMBERSHIPS BY OCCUPATION[a]

NUMBER OF MEMBERSHIPS	Professional & technical	Managers & proprietors	Clerical & sales	Skilled	Semi-skilled	Un-skilled	Unem-ployed	Totals %	N
None	12	44	31	51	59	62	63	56.2	(609)[b]
One	5	22	31	32	23	22	19	21.7	(235)
Two	12	20	25	13	13	9	11	11.6	(126)
Three	24	3	9	4	3	5	2	5.1	(55)
Four	11	3	3	—	3	2	2	2.8	(30)
Five or more	35	7	—	—	—	—	2	2.7	(29)
Total	99 (57)[b]	99 (59)	99 (32)	100 (85)	101 (191)	100 (519)	99 (141)	100.1	(1084)

OCCUPATION

[a] Two cases lost due to nonresponses.
[b] Figures in parentheses refer to number of cases.

Average wages may amount to more than that, but so far as personal wellbeing is concerned, there is little more than a difference in the form of insecurity. We expect, therefore, to find that a considerable part of the distinction between the unemployed and the unskilled is due to theoretically extraneous features, such as variation of the sex composition of the categories.

In order to facilitate handling large amounts of data, all white-collar occupation types were aggregated. These are: professional, technical and kindred; proprietors, managers, and officials; clerical and sales; and one farm owner who lived in the city. Within the white-collar category, the professional and technical have significantly more voluntary association memberships than either managers, proprietors and officials, or clerical and sales workers. The white-collar set, as a whole, however, is clearly different from the blue-collar workers. In the analysis that follows we shall treat the white-collar workers as a unit, unless the evidence suggests that explanation of relationships would be furthered by separate analysis.

The blue-collar workers were divided into two sets. High blue-collar workers consist of the skilled and semiskilled (or operatives). Low blue-collar workers are manual or unskilled workers, including as a major component 45 domestic workers (44 females and 1 male) who for some purposes will be studied as a manual-labor group having special characteristics. Those 141 persons who were not working are not listed among the three other sets, and thus when we speak of white-collar, high blue-collar, or low blue-collar workers, we are concerned with them in their current work status.

Education usually is highly correlated with occupational status, and therefore we would expect education to be highly correlated with voluntary association membership. We may

not assume, however, that this relationship between education and occupation is analogous in all particulars to that for
whites; education has less utility for Negroes than for whites
in producing favorable life chances.

The general results regarding education may be treated
briefly here. We find the expected positive correlation between education and voluntary association membership. The
data are presented in Table 2. The distinctions in membership
due to higher education do not become marked until the college level, where the categories need to be extended beyond
five or more before the mode is reached among college graduates (see column 16+).

TABLE 2

EDUCATION AND VOLUNTARY ASSOCIATION MEMBERSHIP

	YEARS OF FORMAL EDUCATION				
NUMBER OF MEMBERSHIPS	0–6 %	7–9 %	10–11 %	12–15 %	16+ %
None	63.9	62.7	61.5	46.6	4.0
One	21.7	22.0	19.1	26.9	8.0
Two	9.9	9.5	13.1	14.8	10.0
Three or more	4.5	5.8	6.3	11.7	78.0
Total	100.0	100.0	100.0	100.0	100.0
N	(222)	(295)	(252)	(264)	(50)

Other measures of status and some personal categorical
attributes typically show correlation with voluntary association membership, but are not theoretically significant in our
analysis.[6] Six such categories are displayed in Table 3. Some
of these are factors that make a person categorically eligible

TABLE 3

VOLUNTARY ASSOCIATION MEMBERSHIPS BY STATUS
AND PERSONAL CATEGORICAL ATTRIBUTES

| | MEMBERSHIP IN PERCENTS | | | | | Totals | |
	None	One	Two	Three	Four or more	%	N
Status within family							
Head	56	22	12	5	5	100	(1,036)
Not head	49	25	6	8	12	100	(49)
Sex							
Male	59	21	11	5	4	100	(726)
Female	51	22	14	5	8	100	(359)
Age							
20–29	61	22	8	5	4	100	(183)
30–39	61	17	10	7	5	100	(302)
40–49	58	23	14	3	2	100	(291)
50–60	48	25	13	6	8	100	(291)

TABLE 3 (Continued)

| | MEMBERSHIP IN PERCENTS | | | | | Totals | |
	None	One	Two	Three	Four or more	%	N
Housing							
Rent	67	20	9	3	1	100	(514)
Own	46	23	15	7	9	100	(556)
Residence in years							
Less than one	76	16	5	2	1	100	(171)
One to four	56	22	11	5	6	100	(361)
Five or more	49	24	14	6	7	100	(529)
Place of Origin							
Local	54	19	12	6	9	100	(412)
Other Florida	51	27	12	5	5	100	(272)
Other U.S.	60	21	11	5	3	100	(390)
Non-U.S.	70	30	0	0	0	100	(10)

for membership but are not causes of membership. In other words, they are necessary but not sufficient reasons for membership. For example, owning a home is a necessary condition for joining a homeowners' association, but by itself does not allow a prediction of membership. Similarly, sex is a criterion of membership in a single-sex organization (e.g., a women's club) but being a woman does not allow a prediction that a woman will join a women's club. Thus, a higher percentage of homeowners than of renters belong to at least one voluntary association (due to the meaning of ownership in Tampa) but we do not believe ownership (or sex) are strategic independent sociological variables.

It is also the case that long-term residents more often belonged to voluntary associations. Length of residence refers to the amount of time a person has lived in a specific dwelling, measured in categories of less than one year, one to four years, and five years or more. We would expect this measure to be only sluggishly related to variation in membership. A more socially meaningful concept would be required for the results to account for the personal significance of the community of residence. A family's memberships are likely to be affected only if it moves beyond access to certain known organizations or beyond the influence of specific social bonds that cause joining. On the other hand, although moving may not be a sufficient causal factor in limiting membership, frequent moving may be an indicator of other things that by themselves are related to membership, such as poverty or family dismemberment. We concluded that length of residence was one of many intervening or marginal variables to our research problem—real, but unimportant for the problem at hand.

Membership varied little with age. Homeownership,

length of residence, and age are, of course, interrelated. The older the person, the more likely he will have lived continuously in the same dwelling and the more likely he will own the building. Age, however, is not colinear with ownership and length of residence as to voluntary association membership, since people usually begin to curtail memberships when they retire and they do so even earlier for those voluntary associations that are related to the child-rearing years. In the retirement years people don't often belong regardless of their homeownership or length of residence.

Categorical distinctions about place of birth are simple research variables that have predictable consequences, the most reliable of which is that rural residents belong to voluntary associations less frequently. There is apparently a general southward migration of Negroes in Florida, in which cities unlike those of the old South serve as major attractions: Tampa on the gulf coast, Miami, West Palm Beach, and Fort Lauderdale on the Atlantic coast, among others. There is a saying in Florida that goes something like this: "The souther you go the norther you get." In any case, Tampa apparently attracts many southern Negroes from nearby states, for reasons that probably differ from those of migrating whites. Negroes probably come because Tampa is more northern in its racial and employment characteristics; whites come because of the climate and the romance of it all. We found almost no cases of northward Negro migration to Tampa. We do not have information about exact age at migration, but most respondents were able to name a place where they spent their childhood (data not shown). There was a slightly lower rate of membership for people of rural than urban origin, but most of the urban ones were local residents. As was the case with the other attributes, the meaning of place of origin and rearing is difficult to determine, since it is associated with other factors such as education and occupational status. The latter, in general, prove to be more discriminating, sociologically.

Before turning to a test of the thesis one further comment is in order about this class of attributes. In addition to the characteristics already mentioned, four-fifths of the professional and technical white-collar workers were raised in a large city, whereas more than half of the low blue-collar were raised in a small city or in a rural area. The remainder of the white-collar fall in an intermediate position. We will not formally take up the subject of job mobility, but these data suggest a three-generation sequence of migration from rural areas and small towns to larger towns and finally to large cities. This does not mean that persons never migrate directly from rural areas to large cities, but rather that job mobility possibly is linked to a different migration pattern. Of course, the number who negotiate this sequence is limited and we must recognize those whose success takes a different course. If this kind of job mobility takes three generations (and there is other evidence that it does) and if urbanization takes place rapidly enough to interrupt the experience of the intermediate step of living in smaller towns, job mobility may be slowed. If it is true that the mobility career of important community leaders is as we have described it, one of the basic problems of southern Negro communities can be pinpointed: the rapid urbanization of southern Negroes has exceeded the rate at which qualified professionals are produced to provide leadership, at least so far as voluntary associations are concerned.

All things considered, occupation is the most crucial variable, and it is occupation to which we shall give greatest attention.

MEMBERSHIP AND SOCIAL RELATIONSHIPS AT WORK

Although all of the variables or attributes presented in Table 3 are related to membership in voluntary associations, an important question remains: So what? In chapter 1 we suggested that research on voluntary associations has essentially failed because it has not asked important questions, i.e., it has too often been restricted to questions (like those we have just answered) that have limited theoretical relevance. In light of the demonstrated statistical correlation of voluntary association membership and occupation, one might inquire further for the causes of membership in the social nature of work itself. One might ask: How is it possible for the normative forces of the social relationships at work to have pluralistic consequences in the community, away from the place and time of work?[7] A more concrete question is how the tasks themselves generate social relations leading to norms or values that serve to promote pluralistic consequences. As mentioned in chapter 1, some work directly generates joining as a specific requirement of holding a job; more typically the organization of work has indirect consequences for joining. Generally, there is a complex set of interrelated work characteristics, some of which generate reasons to join voluntary associations or, in other words, have "pluralistic consequences."

This complexity is why we use occupation as a statistical control, having demonstrated its basic relationship to membership. Moreover, we do not consider that the social relations in employment "explain" all of the variation in voluntary association membership. We will, in fact, indicate some characteristics of communities and occupations that affect voluntary association membership more indirectly and that are not captured by our variables relating to social relations at work. Consequently, it is necessary to control for occupation (i.e., to hold occupation constant) in order to eliminate both the effects of differences of occupational status and the influence of those additional variables associated with it.

The social relationships of work have several dimensions; one we labeled coracialism; another, collegiality; another, reinforcement. As we have noted, other dimensions may be identified, but we plan here to examine only those we consider basic; our list of social relations is not exhaustive.

Ignoring for the moment the occupational status of the respondent, we see that our data (presented in Table 4) show a positive overall relationship between joining and coracialism. Those with high coracialism more often join than do those with low or medium. Let us return for a moment to the basic definition of coracialism, so that the meaning of this will be clear. We did not ask the respondent if his coworkers did support him in specific matters regarding race. Rather we proceeded with questions regarding the more objective characteristics of the work setting, having to do with the presence or absence of Negro coworkers and/or supervisors. Solidarity is an inference, made necessary by the conditions under which interviewing took place, and this should always be kept in mind. The result may then be more fully

TABLE 4

SOCIAL RELATIONSHIPS AND VOLUNTARY ASSOCIATION MEMBERSHIP

	Percent Voluntary Association Membership
Coracialism[a]	
High	60
Medium	39
Low	40
N	(1,039)
Reinforcement	
Yes	48
No	43
N	(1,026)
Collegiality	
Low	44
High	46
N	(1,026)

[a] These differences are statistically significant.

stated in terms of the components of the measure: the Negro is most likely to join voluntary associations when he works under a Negro supervisor and therefore also enjoys coracialism. The table reveals no difference in membership between those who have a white supervisor and Negro coworkers and those who have neither a white supervisor nor Negro coworkers. Later in this chapter we will explore factors that will add precision to the finding, as well as factors that may be responsible for the similarity of membership between the moderate and low coracialism categories.

Reinforcement was defined as the opportunity to call

upon certain kinds of outside power at work, and was operationalized in terms of the presence or absence of union or civil-service membership. We did not ask about the effectiveness of the outside power, but only about its categorical existence. It was predicted (hypothesis 2) that reinforcement would be related to membership in Negro-rights voluntary associations but not in other voluntary associations. Since we are concerned in this chapter only with voluntary associations in general, without regard to type, we would expect only a weak relationship to be found because only a fraction (10 percent) of the memberships in the community are in Negro-rights organizations. This proves to be the case: reinforcement is not related to membership in voluntary associations. Hypothesis 2 is verified for the total sample. Later, when we analyze voluntary associations by type, it will be possible to examine Negro-rights organizations alone.

Collegiality was defined in terms of the informal ties of a worker to his coworkers. We asked two questions: "Do many of your close friends work at the same place you work?" and "Do you talk to the people you work with away from work?" These questions were combined into an index that differentiates those whose work experiences apparently are isolated from their nonwork experiences from those for whom the experiences are tied together. In addition, since those who work alone cannot experience collegiality, we separately identified persons who claimed that they worked alone.

We found no relationship between collegiality and joining within the total sample. This result is in accord with hypothesis 3 that collegiality is not related to joining, but should prove to strengthen the other relationships. This finding takes on added significance when the relationship between collegiality and coracialism is examined. That relationship is significant. In other words, those with high collegiality more often have high coracialism than do those with low collegiality. Obviously, this overall relationship might be spurious because there could be no coracialism for those who work alone and therefore have no collegiality. However, eliminating from the sample those who have no collegiality because they work alone does not alter the relationship between coracialism and collegiality.

Coracialism is logically possible with only one Negro coworker, in which case collegiality is also possible, but the likelihood of friendship is not the same with only one available person as when the number of possible choices is quite large. We will take up this matter of size of place of work later in the chapter.

In summary, the relationship between coracialism and collegiality is independent of the relationship between joining and either of these variables taken singly. The results support hypothesis 1 that coracialism is related to joining, even though coracialism and collegiality are themselves positively related. Even though the explanation appears to be correct for the entire sample it may be that the significant relation of collegiality and coracialism is not the same at each level. Indeed, variations in coracialism alone at each status level would lead us to expect such distinctions.[8] Therefore, we turn to examination of these variables within each occupational category.

OCCUPATIONAL STATUS
AND SOCIAL RELATIONS

The variation in the social relations among occupations may be observed in Table 5. The most striking variation is in coracialism. Three-fifths of the white-collar respondents have high coracialism, and three-fifths of the high blue-collar have medium coracialism. The low blue-collar respondents are somewhat more evenly distributed among the coracialism categories than are the high blue-collar. In concrete terms, this means that the white-collar, more often than others, work in settings where they have Negro supervisors and Negro coworkers. The high blue-collar, on the other hand, tend to work in settings where they have Negro coworkers but white supervisors. There is not as much variation in reinforcement among occupations, although the percentage with reinforcement tends to increase slightly as occupational status decreases.

A more complex pattern is found for collegiality. White-collar and low blue-collar have the higher proportions of isolated workers, with almost one-fifth of the low blue-collar in this category. At the other extreme, two-thirds of the high blue-collar have high collegiality.

Since we have found that coracialism and occupational status are each positively related to joining, the extent to which these factors are indicators of the same thing, rather than independent of one another, should be determined. This is important for our theory, for if the frequently made as-

TABLE 5

SOCIAL RELATIONS VARIABLES AND OCCUPATION

	White-collar %	High blue-collar %	Low blue-collar %
Coracialism			
High	61	8	18
Medium	19	59	45
Low	20	33	37
Total	100	100	100
	(147)[a]	(276)	(516)
Reinforcement			
Yes	14	19	22
No	86	81	78
Total	100	100	100
	(146)	(272)	(511)
Collegiality			
Works alone	12	7	18
Low	35	27	32
High	53	66	50
Total	100	100	100
	(141)	(274)	(512)

[a] Figures in parentheses refer to total number of cases.

sumption that status is the only explanation of membership is adequate, then when status is held constant, the effects of coracialism should disappear statistically.

This could be tested in alternate ways: each level of coracialism could be examined to see if status differences within it are correlated with joining; or status could be held constant to see if variations in coracialism for each status are associated with significant differences in joining. Because occupational status measures are better known and are relatively standardized in research literature, we have chosen to examine the relationships between voluntary association membership and coracialism for each occupational category. When we examine each category, if we find a significant association between coracialism and joining we will conclude that we have discovered an independent source of voluntary association membership.

Given the observed variation among occupations in reinforcement and collegiality, and in joining as well, it seems necessary to explore the possibility of a relationship of reinforcement and collegiality with joining, within each occupational category. Following previous reasoning, a weaker relationship between reinforcement and joining is expected because reinforcement is related only to joining the Negro-rights component of the total. We do not expect collegiality to be directly related to joining within any of the occupational sets.

Among respondents with white-collar jobs, we found a positive relationship between coracialism and joining (see Table 6). Those with high and medium coracialism are more likely to belong to voluntary associations than are those with low coracialism.

Among high blue-collar respondents, there also was an association between coracialism and joining. When the results were examined in detail, however, it was found that the association was irregular. Those with medium coracialism were more likely to have no memberships, whereas those with low coracialism had a higher number than expected in the category of two or more memberships. Such irregularity is typical of high blue-collar workers and is an issue to which we shall

TABLE 6

PERCENT BELONGING TO ONE OR MORE VOLUNTARY
ASSOCIATION, BY OCCUPATION AND SOCIAL RELATIONS

	OCCUPATION AND SOCIAL RELATIONS		
	White-collar %	High blue-collar %	Low blue-collar %
Coracialism			
High	78 (90)[a]	76 (21)	51 (94)
Medium	89 (28)	38 (165)	35 (232)
Low	41 (29)	46 (89)	37 (190)
	*	*	*
Reinforcement			
Yes	75 (20)	51 (53)	40 (112)
No	72 (126)	42 (219)	38 (399)
Collegiality			
Works alone	53 (17)	40 (20)	36 (90)
Low	64 (50)	49 (74)	43 (164)
High	87 (74)	42 (180)	38 (259)
	*		

* Statistically significant.
[a] Figures in parentheses represent number of cases in the base.

return. In any event, it is apparent that those with high co-racialism join more often than do those with low or medium. The predicted relationship between coracialism and joining also was found among low blue-collar workers with the same irregularity in details as noted for the high blue-collar.

Both the low and the high blue-collar results indicate a tendency for those with low coracialism to belong to two or more voluntary associations somewhat more often than would be expected on the basis of chance alone. Table 6 shows for the white-collar worker a large percentage gap between the low and the medium coracialism categories, whereas for the blue-collar the large gap is between the medium and high. This indicates that greater coracialism is required to back up membership among the blue-collar workers.

Coracialism then, operates (with qualifications yet to be explained) independently of occupational status to produce pluralistic consequences. This basic aspect of the theory is established. What of collegiality and reinforcement?

Reinforcement was not related to membership in voluntary associations within any of the occupational categories.[9] These results are in accord with our earlier argument that reinforcement should not be related to overall memberships, although we did expect reinforcement to be associated with membership in militant and other Negro-rights organizations. This topic will be examined at length in chapter 4.

No relationship was found between collegiality and joining for either low blue-collar or high blue-collar workers. But, contrary to hypothesis 3, there was a significant relationship between collegiality and joining for white-collar workers. If our reasoning in chapter 1 was correct, this indicates that there are conditions in the work situation of white-collar, but not blue-collar workers, that made collegiality more than a means of strengthening other social relations that encourage membership. Why should this be the case?

The most prevalent white-collar occupation is teaching. The visitor to the research area soon notices the exceptional demands made upon teachers for leadership. They are categorically high in education because of the requirements of the school board that teachers have a college degree, and derivatively of high importance in the community, which lacks educated leaders. They are typically stable in residence and, it will be recalled, length of residence is correlated with high membership rates. Teachers are salaried, which adds to their stability. Teachers may have an added source of extra-systematic power, that of academic tenure, which is obtained after three years of service (we did not include this measure in the reinforcement index).[10] There are a number of professional voluntary associations that teachers are encouraged to join by colleagues and in many cases by supervisors as well. Since school desegregation at the time of data-gathering was not extensive, most Negro teachers had Negro supervisors and colleagues and were thus automatically in our high coracialism category. In addition, at the time of the study, teachers' professional associations were becoming militant vis à vis the school board and legislature. The teachers' organizations apparently enjoyed help from a majority of teachers as well as principals, and we would expect those teachers with higher collegiality to be more exposed to pressures to join. These comments indicate the existence of multiple bonds in work and community that are tapped by the collegiality index (which indicates both reported interaction at work and friendships at work that extend to the community).

Three kinds of additional empirical tests were employed in an effort to explore the association of collegiality with membership among white-collar workers. First, when white-collar workers were separated into nonprofessionals (i.e., managers, proprietors and officials, as well as clerical and sales workers, who do not differ significantly as to membership rates) and professionals (mostly teachers), we found that collegiality was associated with membership rates only for professionals, and that most professionals had high coracialism as well. Second, when white-collar workers were classified as to self-employed and company or bureaucratic (distinctions that will be explained more fully later), it was found that the self-employed white-collar workers had proportionately fewer memberships than the company-employed.[11] Third, we found that the size of the organization for which the white-collar person worked was associated with membership rates: the larger the organization, the higher the rate of joining. Since large organizations make collegiality possible and likely on a probability basis alone, this again draws our attention to the collegiality factor, but ties it in with teachers, who are the largest single category of white-collar workers employed by large organizations.

In summary, coracialism proves to be related to voluntary association membership when occupational status is held constant, reinforcement is not related to voluntary association membership, and collegiality is related to voluntary association membership only among white-collar respondents. That the relationship of collegiality with membership required supplementary explanation suggests the need for further and more systematic exploration of the variables utilized in these explanations. Moreover, there are possible other social relations than coracialism, reinforcement, and collegiality. We turn therefore to a more thorough consideration of the nature of the employer as a factor in voluntary association memberships of workers.

MEMBERSHIP AND
THE EMPLOYER

One objective in examining types of employers is to sharpen our understanding of coracialism, reinforcement, and collegiality as causes of voluntary association membership. The categories selected regarding the employer should have the quality of including a given organization once only, and should reflect those features that most sharply delineate employers as to kinds of social relations. In chapter 1, we focused attention on certain employment settings that were of particular significance for the Negro worker. We found it useful to differentiate between the company-employed, the self-employed, and the person-employed, and these categories will be used in this chapter. In addition, we occasionally will find it useful to differentiate the company-employed by the number of employees of the company.

These types of employers typically have different degrees of authority. We consider the self-employed to be the least and the person-employed the most subject to immediate demands of authority. The company-employed occupy an intermediate position. We also expect occupational status variations to the extent to which these differentiate the respondents. In addition, these types of employment are important for reasons other than authority.

The reasons for selecting self-employed, person-employed, and company-employed are practical as well as theoretical. We found in our pilot studies that the knowledge that less educated workers had of their employers was very limited. In some cases they did not know the name of their employer. Some only knew the name of the person who paid them. We therefore had to exclude some important factual questions, and instead asked a number of things from which inferences could be made, when necessary, about the source of authority and the size of the work force.

Self-employed is a term that many workers apply to themselves when they perceive that the interpersonal relations of the interview situation require elevation of their prestige. Interviewers were instructed to ask if the person habitually contracted his own work, obtained his own living by seeking clients, and had a high degree of responsibility for the success or failure of the enterprise. The criteria were highly pragmatic and were used essentially to guard against the tendencies to mistakenly place the respondent in one of the other two categories. Yet, to a considerable extent, the self-employed and person-employed sets are real alternative classifications for many persons, and not just a matter of prestige-claiming in the interview.

Person-employed included a fairly large number of clear cases of traditional Negro employment, such as domestic or household labor, or casual manual labor in the service of an individual small businessman. Domestics who frequently worked for different employers each day tended repeatedly to speak with some pride of themselves as self-employed, but were not so classified unless they did labor in their own homes for others. Some distinguishing features of the latter type of employment are control of the conditions of work, the relation of work and home, and freedom from control by a single employer or client.

Company-employed referred to work for a company or corporate firm or bureaucratic organization, whether or not for profit. Schools and hospitals are companies. As noted before, some workers have very limited knowledge of their employers. Consequently they will claim that they are person-employed when in fact they work for a company. We tried to identify these cases, but the possibility remains that some respondents classified as person-employed are employed by a company.

Employment Patterns and Membership Patterns

Fourteen percent of those who were working were person-employed (almost all of whom were low blue-collar workers). The company-employed comprised 79 percent of those working. In contrast, only 7 percent were classified as self-employed.

As was noted in chapter 1, most of the self-employed are proprietors or entrepreneurial professionals, while a few are blue-collar businessmen. The self-employed are a mixed lot, widely separated in community prestige. They are similar as to the structure of their relationships to others, in that all have clients and business responsibilities. Some have a few employees. Since this group is small, it will not be possible to analyze them extensively.

The person- and company-employed have about the same percentage who belong to at least one voluntary association (33 and 34 percent, respectively). The self-employed, however, have a higher percentage who belong to at least one voluntary association (57 percent). Since almost all of the self-employed are white-collar, this result could be expected on the basis of what we have already shown about white-collar workers. This finding, in addition, points to the necessity of considering the three types of employment by occupational status levels.

When this is done, it is found that only company-employed have enough cases at all levels to warrant examination of subcategories. That is, the types of employed are numerically class biased: person-employed are biased toward lower status, self-employed are biased toward higher status, and only the company-employed are fairly evenly distributed by occupational status (although even here there is a slight distortion, as the high blue-collar set is somewhat more heavily weighted toward the company-employed).

Company-Employed in Detail

We found a positive association between occupational status and voluntary association membership for company-employed respondents. When the distribution of memberships by status is examined in detail (see Table 7) the strong effect of white-collar worker can be seen. In fact, the table does not extend far enough to expose the mode for the white-collar workers. When the relationships between joining and coracialism, reinforcement, and collegiality are examined (males only) again only the white-collar workers are prominent.[12] Coracialism and membership are positively associated for white-collar, company-employed males but not for all company-employed males. Reinforcement is inversely associated with membership.[13]

The only other statistically significant relationship is that between coracialism and membership for the high blue-collar males. It will be recalled that when the total sample was considered without distinguishing types of employers, coracialism was related to membership among both the high and low

TABLE 7

VOLUNTARY ASSOCIATION MEMBERSHIPS AMONG
COMPANY-EMPLOYED WORKERS, BY
TYPE OF OCCUPATION

| TYPE OF OCCUPATION | MEMBERSHIPS IN PERCENTS | | | |
	0	1	2+	Total
White-collar	17 (15)[a]	17 (15)	67 (60)	100 (90)
High blue-collar	57 (153)	25 (67)	19 (50)	100 (270)
Low blue-collar	64 (246)	22 (85)	14 (54)	100 (385)
Total	55.5 (414)	22.5 (167)	22.0 (164)	100 (745)

[a] Figures in parentheses refer to the number of cases in the base.

blue-collar workers. Among low blue-collar, company-employed females, those with high coracialism belong more often than do those with low or medium.

Self-Employed, Person-Employed, and Company-Employed

Two comparisons with the company-employed are worth noting. Self-employed white-collar workers have a lower percentage of members of one or more organizations than do the white-collar company-employed (56 and 83 percent, respectively).[14] This important finding will be examined in chapter 4, when we consider the specific organizations that Negro businessmen join and why they appear to join so few.

The second comparison is that the low blue-collar person-employed have a higher rate of membership than the company-employed (44 percent and 36 percent, respectively), although this difference does not reach statistical significance.

The first finding was explained previously, and is consistent with our finding concerning coracialism, collegiality, and reinforcement of the white-collar worker. The second result, however, seems to refute hypothesis 1, since we would expect that person-employed workers would frequently work alone or for white employers and thus lack coracialism, as well as collegiality and reinforcement (union membership). This finding takes on added significance since it involves a large portion of the sample.

The difference in membership patterns of these low blue-collar persons is perhaps due to the composition of the categories of person-employed and company-employed. Most person-employed are women and most company-employed are men. Since women generally have a higher rate of membership we could expect to find these results reversed or at least diminished if we considered only a male subsample (supposing that the female rate of membership was due to causes other than those examined as dependent variables). This does not prove to be the case: in fact, the difference in membership between person-employed and company-employed among males is even greater than among all low blue-collar respondents and now reaches statistical significance. However, the few low blue-collar female company-employed belong somewhat more often than do the female person-employed, although these differences are not statistically significant.

Comparing the results for males with those for females, the male company-employed belong less often than do the female company-employed, although the person-employed males belong more often that the person-employed females. Using females as our basis of comparison. we have a choice here of arguing either that male person-employed "over-belong," that male company-employed "underbelong," or both. Since we normally expect males to belong less often than females, it seems appropriate to conclude that male person-employed workers belonging more than male company-employed can be considered overbelonging.

This interpretation makes sense in other ways as well. The male person-employed is a less readily identified category in research than is the female person-employed, half of whom are occupied at day's work. Although we recognize that there are person-employed males, such as street-corner pickup workers, helpers for free-lance carpenters, and the like, the category still is often self-defined by the respondent. Thus, we would expect a variety of mistakes to be made by the respondent in the identification of his employment category.[15]

Another check on this issue is to examine coracialism as it relates to voluntary association memberships. Coracialism appears to be positively related to voluntary association membership within the categories of both the person-employed and the company-employed, although neither quite reaches statistical significance. Thus although the company-employed overall have lower membership than the person-employed, our coracialism hypothesis is not refuted. Coracialism is more clearly related to voluntary association membership among the person-employed. The fact that one-fifth of the person-employed claimed some coracialism suggests the merit of our earlier concern that these respondents may not know for whom they work. Although our findings that one-fifth of the person-employed enjoy at least Negro coworkers (and that 12 percent have not only Negro coworkers but a Negro supervisor as well) may be correct, these findings also may indicate errors.

It is not our purpose to explain exhaustively variations

associated with type of employer. It is obvious that there is a rich source of material here yet to be mined. In particular, the type of employer seems to be of crucial importance in explaining the extensive pluralism of company-employed professionals and the mass society orientation of unskilled and manual workers. The strong explanatory power of type of employer even as an admittedly gross structural variable, lies in the amount and, derivatively, the kind of interaction it makes possible, and therefore it modifies coracialism and collegiality.

MEMBERSHIP AND PERSONAL CHARACTERISTICS

In Table 3 we presented gross membership data for a number of common characteristics of persons, which were correlated with membership but were not strategic as research variables. In this section we will trace in greater detail the relationship of some of the personal characteristics to membership. The main issue, again, is that these attributes make people selectively accessible to the operation of the variables of coracialism, reinforcement, and collegiality, and may therefore be seen as analogous to the effect of type of employment.

We noted earlier that while white-collar and low blue-collar sets were composed of about one-third females, the proportion of females for the high blue-collar was much smaller. Since the results for the high blue-collar category are not always in accord with our hypothesis, restricting the analysis to males may help only in interpretation of these results. Moreover, by restricting our analysis for the moment to male heads of households, we gain the additional advantage of purifying our concepts of coracialism, reinforcement, collegiality, and type of employment, since these concepts may have different implications for men than for women.[16] A further specification also seems in order: since heads of households may have different patterns of membership and commitment in the community than nonheads, the following statements will apply to male heads of households only.[17]

The relationship previously found between occupational status and voluntary association membership is maintained. The results for male heads disclose results quite similar to those of the total sample, except that male white-collar respondents belong somewhat less frequently than do female white-collar respondents (see Table 8).[18]

We have pointed out before that coracialism, reinforcement, and collegiality do not exhaust the list of relationships leading a person to join voluntary associations, and that some of the important sources are not directly related to work, even though factors such as occupational status might show high rates of covariance. Thus it might be asked whether the extent of interaction in the community leads to the development of social relationships that result in membership, as does interaction at work.

We have argued that collegiality at work is not decisive as a determinant of joining, but is indirectly related through coracialism. In the same sense, informal social relations off the job would not operate directly to encourage voluntary association memberships because there is nothing in the goals of informal social groups that might be furthered by membership. This is in sharp contrast to the groupings at

TABLE 8

VOLUNTARY ASSOCIATION MEMBERSHIPS
FOR MALE HEADS OF HOUSEHOLDS

	MEMBERSHIPS IN PERCENTS			
TYPE OF OCCUPATION	None	One	Two or more	Total
White-collar	35 (29)[a]	18 (18)	47 (54)	100
High blue-collar	57 (57)	26 (25)	17 (18)	100
Low blue-collar	65 (62)	20 (22)	15 (16)	100

[a] Corresponding percentage of total sample, both male and female, included in parentheses.

work, where voluntary association membership may be important to the goals of the work group or the employer. We do not deny that formal associations may spring from an informal setting, but we find such actions to be not very imperative or numerous. Friendship or collegiality establishes the necessary links for social influence transmission, but by itself supplies no imperative to any particular kind of joining.

We provided for a general test of this collateral hypothesis by asking respondents about the frequency with which they visited friends and relatives. There was no association between this informal visiting and voluntary association membership. Of respondents with at least one voluntary association membership, 59 percent report that they often visit friends and relatives, but 55 percent of those who do not belong often visit also. This negative finding was true for the total membership of respondents, as well as for each specific type of voluntary association, which seems to discount the obvious possibility that informal recreational or expressive associations would be related to informal visiting. We shall return to this matter of type of voluntary association in chapters 3 and 4.

When examined for each occupational status level, there is only a weak relationship between formal voluntary association membership and visiting.

Is collegiality related to visiting friends and relatives? Since we found only a relationship between collegiality and membership among white-collar workers, and no relationship between visiting and membership in this group, the correlation between collegiality and visiting is indifferent so far as the collateral hypothesis is concerned.

MASS MAN AND
PLURALIST MAN: PORTRAITS

Up to this point we have been examining associations among theoretical concepts. Here, we focus attention on the individuals enmeshed in these forces. The data are not different, although the perspective is. The task is to highlight features of the "mass man" and the "pluralist man." We define the mass man (male or female) operationally as one who belongs to no voluntary associations, while the pluralist man is one who belongs to two or more. In our sample there are 609 mass men and 240 pluralist men. In the comparisons we will consider the differences as well as the similarities between these types. Supplementary tables in Appendix B may aid the reader in interpretation of this summary.

Since the sample is weighted toward heads of households, it is not surprising that most mass men as well as most pluralist men are heads (95 percent). There are somewhat more males among mass men than among pluralist men (70 percent to 61 percent). Pluralist men tend to be somewhat older than mass men, as well as to have more coracialism. Pluralist man is much more likely to be white-collar than mass man, and more often has at least a high-school education. Pluralist man has more often lived five or more years at his present address than has mass man.

Considering the occupational distribution of mass and pluralist men, we find reflections of our findings about the differential effects of social relationships: mass man has lower occupational status (or is unemployed) and therefore has infrequent high coracialism, i.e., he works alone or among groups of Negroes, but under white supervision. Pluralist man sometimes works alone but his most striking characteristic is that he has Negro supervision and Negro coworkers. The pluralist man has official backing and security from within the organization: mass man has his fellow workers but only formal title to outside help. The pluralist is an insider; the mass man is an outsider, and because (scarce) education is his principal means of mobility, he is likely to remain so.

SUMMARY

We now have looked at the gross tests of the hypotheses. It is apparent that while we have not failed to find some confirmation, neither have we completely succeeded. In part this may be due to the fact that we have treated membership too grossly: we need to make distinctions among the voluntary associations to which Negroes belong. Accordingly, in the next two chapters, membership in types of voluntary associations will be examined.

The descriptive task becomes substantial, and so we will not return to the subject of this chapter until we reach chapter 4.

NOTES

1. Murray Hausknecht, *The Joiners: A Sociological Description of Voluntary Association Membership in the United States,* p. 62.

2. Nicholas Babchuk and Ralph V. Thompson, "Voluntary Associations of Negroes," *American Sociological Review* 27: 647–655.

3. Charles R. Wright and Herbert H. Hyman, "Voluntary Association Memberships of American Adults: Evidence from National Samples," *American Sociological Review* 23:290.

4. Hausknecht cites a number of national studies in which higher status, as indicated by education, income, and occupation, is associated with higher rates of membership. See Hausknecht, *The Joiners,* pp. 23–25. The race of respondent is not identified in these figures but there is no reason to expect race to be a factor in variation in membership by status.

5. Whenever we make a concluding statement about a relationship of the kind made here (i.e., "The more —, the more—") we have made a statistical test for significance, and the conventional $p < .05$ has been found. Hypothetical statements of this logical form do not imply symmetry: "The more the A, the more the B" is not necessarily reversible. Unless the numerical

results are of general interest, or speculation about the nature of a statistical method or result is related to the conclusions we have made, no mention will be made of the numerical result. The method used is typical of field research. Data was punched on IBM cards, and tests of significance (numbering in the thousands) were calculated by computer.

6. Family life cycles or phases that are related to voluntary association memberships have analogies in work careers. At one point in a work career, a person may be expected to participate, while a short time later participation might be judged inappropriate or pretentious. These cycles may coincide. Thus if a boss has decided that at forty a junior executive has gone about as far as he is going to go in the firm, those social clubs and business memberships related to advancement are suddenly out of the question. The investment capitalism of voluntary associations is typical of the ascendant slope of the career—when the plateau is reached, it is time to curtail social investment. Often the child-rearing years, with their demand for community participation (PTA, Boy Scouts, church youth work, and so on) end about the same time as the advancement phase of work.

7. In Seymour M. Lipset, Martin Trow and J. S. Coleman's *Union Democracy,* which we discussed in chapter 1, the high rate of voluntary association memberships concerned only those among members of the same union or same shop. These associations were directly structured by ecological features, interaction requirements on the job, common time off, and so on. We are concerned here with something more general: how do the social relations of *any* kind of work have pluralistic consequences, of which the *"union democracy"* is a special and unique case?

8. The comment of Blalock on this design problem is apropos: ". . . . whenever supposedly independent variables are highly intercorrelated, it becomes difficult to disentangle their component effects. Sampling errors are likely to be quite large, and inferences risky" (Hubert M. Blalock, Jr., *Toward a Theory of Minority-Group Relations,* p. 4).

9. High blue-collar respondents with reinforcement joined

two or more voluntary associations more often than expected; those without reinforcement joined one only or did not join. However, our only concern here is with the effect of the social relations at work on joining or not joining (i.e., no memberships, in contrast with at least one membership). We also note that in every occupational category those with coracialism more often join than do those without.

10. We call this "outside power" or "extrasystemic" because the culture that supports it is outside the bureaucratic system. Moreover, tenure is presumably won through action by the employee, not by the school system. Other professional workers who are similar to teachers and are included in this category of analysis do not have formal protection similar to tenure. They include welfare workers and administrative workers with college degrees, who are less numerous than the teachers.

11. This finding would probably surprise most people who know the Negro community. There is a common image of the doctors, lawyers, dentists, morticians, and clergy as leaders who are active in community affairs. Indeed, one might conclude this from our discussion in chapter 1. There are several reasons for this misperception. It may well be that these people are prominent and do have power, but we found in our sample that they are few. In addition, the frequency of belonging to voluntary associations does not necessarily reflect prominence, power, or the strategic location of the organizations to which the person belongs.

12. For some later purposes, it will be desirable to examine the social relationships of work among male respondents only. In order to avoid repeating a number of statements we will adopt the procedure here of presenting results only for males.

13. As we have noted, our reinforcement index fails to include an important source of reinforcement among white-collar workers, that of tenure for teachers. It may be that this omission is the explanation for the finding we have here.

14. Some of this difference in membership between the company-employed and the self-employed may be due to variation

in coracialism, reinforcement, and collegiality, rather than other features of company- and self-employment. To be certain that we are tapping these other features, we must show that appropriate differences remain between the company-employed and the self-employed, within categories of these other concepts.

15. In the data-handling process it was discovered that some respondents answered all the questions designed to be answered by either person- or company-employed, but not by both. As we noted earlier, respondents sometimes did not know for whom they worked, but merely knew who gave the orders, the pay, or both. One may object to the introduction of this type of explanation, but one must remember that there were only nineteen low blue-collar, person-employed males, and consequently a shift of just a few of these respondents could drastically alter the results.

16. When a family is dismembered by male desertion or unexplained absence, the female frequently goes on welfare, usually Aid to Families of Dependent Children. She thus is in the unemployed set. Another typical recourse is for her to work at a flexible occupation, the most frequent of which is domestic service. Another alternative is household merging, often with relatives or parents. The male, on the other hand, does not necessarily leave the sample in this way, for he may be head of another household. It should be recognized that in considering only male heads of households, we are distorting the sample somewhat toward those households that are stable, although the implications of such a distortion are not entirely clear.

17. Of the 727 males in the sample, 718 are heads of households.

18. That "women are joiners" is apparently true, primarily among white-collar respondents. However, it must be remembered that the women in our sample are mostly heads of households, and "adult women" in general are not adequately represented. The forces that structure the voluntary associations of men and of women (as housewives) are quite different, if we consider only the forces of work, which affect men, and the

forces of the home, which affect women. In a certain sense, only some men are white-collar at work, but nearly all house-wives are white-collar in the community. Lacking the specific structuring of their lives at work, which forces men into uni-forms that declare their occupations, women are able to declare themselves more freely as to the roles they wish to claim. In general, we would expect women to encounter less class restric-tion in their voluntary association memberships than men, and this in turn will affect the kind of organizations they form or join. Housewives may be less affected by phase segregation and work imperialism.

3

PATTERNS OF MEMBERSHIP IN A BLACK COMMUNITY

In chapter 2, we considered the sources of variation in the frequency of membership. Obviously there is more to belonging than a simple index of membership rates. We want to know what kind of voluntary associations exist in the black community and what they are like, as well as who joins them. We postpone until chapter 4 the next step of analysis of the association of the work-related research variables of coracialism, reinforcement, and collegiality by status levels with membership in these kinds of organizations.

The word *patterns,* which we have used in the chapter

title, does not adequately convey the complexity of the issues that are involved. Even when simplified by statistical aggregation, the web of relations that we observe is a testimony to the intricate concatenation of human events. To simplify presentation, we will identify three levels of analysis: the person as actor (what groups specific people belong to); voluntary associations in the community (their distribution and the types in the community); the membership in the voluntary association (the distribution of memberships among different kinds of people in the community). Each of these has many aspects. We begin at the level of the organization in the community.

**VOLUNTARY ASSOCIATIONS:
VARIETIES AND TYPES**

The Characteristics of Voluntary Associations

In chapter 1 we provisionally defined the voluntary association as "a formal organization, small or large, in which membership is optional, that is, without compulsion or ascription." It is now appropriate to expand on that definition with some further distinctions.

Voluntary associations are always composed of persons whose identification with the organization is essentially on the basis of shared values regarding some common interest, purpose, or goal. Members are relatively undifferentiated. To put it another way, the differences that do exist are acceptable because they are consistent with goal attainment and are usually dealt with by means of norms that distinguish member roles from roles in the external systems. In contrast are those formal organizations that require that members fill a particular niche in an elaborate division of labor in order to reach an organizational objective and that have authority, that is, legitimated ability to compel performances. The distinction can be made more vivid by contrasting the organization for which the person works and the one he joins in his spare time: one important reason why people join the latter is precisely that the two are in such strong contrast that each offers a motive to perform in the other.

Of course, not all associations that have as their basis the sharing of some common interest are voluntary associations (the army, for instance), only those in which membership is not ascribed or compelled. Although it is something of an oversimplification, many of the most important sociological characteristics that distinguish voluntary associations from nonvoluntary formal organizations are revealed by the distinction between shared values and shared norms respectively. Many organizations that appear to be one type tend to acquire characteristics of the other type in order to deal with certain organizational consequences of specialization.

When common interest is stressed as the sine qua non of voluntary associations, certain other characteristics logically follow. First, they are not "productive" units. Any service or product they may create is a by-product of other activities in which they engage. This is more than a definitional matter: such distinctions, for example, are the basis of tax relief and legal obligations. Voluntary associations are eleemosynary.

Second, voluntary associations are always embedded in a matrix of other types of groups. Moreover, they often grow out of important segments of the division of labor that characterizes the community and the society. This includes the multiple institutional arrangements we have called the emploity. Indeed, our study is based upon such an assumption.

Third, the term *voluntary* indicates there is a choice regarding membership. Consequently, sociologists typically assume that some organizations that are superficially similar to voluntary associations in fact are not voluntary. Unions and churches, for example, have been held to be too ascriptive or compulsory to be treated as voluntary associations.[1]

The Problem of Classification

There have been a number of attempts to classify voluntary associations. Sometimes the result is a set of concrete categories, such as "the PTA," "civic groups," and the like. In such cases, the features of the research problem determine the categories.

The best known abstract formulation concerns *expressive* in contrast to *instrumental.* This typology differentiates voluntary associations in terms of the purpose of membership. Thus, Gordon and Babchuk define instrumental voluntary associations as those that exist "not . . . primarily to furnish activities for members as an end in itself, but to serve as social influence organizations designed to maintain or to create some normative condition change. Such groups exist in order to attain goals that lie outside of the organizations themselves."[2] In other words, they are pressure or vested interest groups, although not all organizations by that name are voluntary associations.

Expressive voluntary associations, on the other hand, are those in which membership is meaningful by virtue of the value to the member of his interaction with other members. An expressive voluntary association is oriented primarily toward interaction among its members, and when it seeks to influence affairs outside itself it does so only to provide for membership continuity (it seeks new members) or to control those things that threaten the pursuit of its internal activities (e.g., a social club may attempt to influence liquor licensing laws, buildings codes, and so on). When organizational survival is dependent on coping with external problems, the structure of the organization may be drastically altered, i.e., it tends to become instrumental. Moreover, a group organized for one purpose (e.g., an expressive voluntary association) will encounter organizational problems with predictable consequences when it attempts a different purpose. Thus what is required in order for an expressive group to deal with instrumental issues is an alteration of structure appropriate to the end sought. Typically, committees or ad hoc groups arise, which gain power in the process of action, leading in turn to cleavages in the group, leadership struggles, and the like. When an organization encounters such problems of survival, it either alters its structure to accommodate its new purposes or it divides into new associations. Thus, over time, any initially pure set gives way to a mixture of impure forms or to organizational differentiation.

In addition, disagreement about typologies of voluntary associations may stem from either the perspective of the observer (whether the focus is on the function of the association or the meaning to the person of membership), or the level of generality attempted. Which perspective is taken should depend upon the problem pursued.

The instrumental-expressive distinction has most often been applied to concrete organizations: association A is instrumental but association B is expressive. Another way of viewing the distinction is to claim that any organization is both an instrumentality for furthering the interests of its members and a vehicle for meeting their expressive needs. Even with this perspective, however, organizations may be held to differ in the primacy of their members' instrumental or expressive interests.[3] On the other hand, we may make the distinction in terms of those characteristics of the organization that are a response to forces outside itself and those that respond to its internal problems. The relationship of the organization to the world about it calls attention to its instrumental problems, while internal maintenance calls attention to its expressive problems.

These examples do not exhaust the possible theoretical distinctions, but we cannot attempt to reconcile these perspectives (if that is possible) nor do we wish to take sides on them. Rather, we have adopted and adapted that which appears useful to our research interest. Accordingly, we will simply classify voluntary associations in terms of their *public* emphasis on either expressive or instrumental goals apart from the meaning of membership to members. In the long run, it would be desirable to distinguish the actual meaning to members of organizations from those announced purposes and values of the organization, but such distinctions involve subtleties that we cannot measure. We will make a first approximation to such an approach in chapter 5 when we distinguish attitudes toward organizations from actions in joining them, and again in chapter 7 when we distinguish attitudes before and after a community crisis.

Selecting Operational Types

In arriving at a final set of ten types of voluntary associations, a series of procedures was used to widen the scope of inquiry to all phases of community organizational life, and then to condense the data into types that were representative of actual distinctions that respondents themselves made in everyday life.[4]

In our first pilot study, sixty students, mostly white, asked Negro respondents if they belonged to any of a list of types of organizations, the names of which were read to the respondent. The interviewer then asked about other memberships. In the present study we found no reason to expand the original list, with the exception of a distinction that became apparent between types of lodges. Imaginary organizations on the list drew almost no responses, which suggests that there was little tendency to inflate or deceive.

A second pilot study involved 300 interviewers from a workshop on poverty. The interviewers, all local teachers, about half Negro and half white, inquired about voluntary associations of the poor, a majority of whom were Negro. The results were compared with a sample of middle-class respondents. The results increased our confidence in our earlier conclusion that we had not missed important organizations or types. As additional checks on inclusiveness, we systematically read the city Negro newspaper for a period of six months. A list of youth social clubs was obtained from the society editor of the paper, and a student in the race relations class of one author asked a Negro night-school class about their memberships. By no means were all of the voluntary associations we discovered mentioned by the respondents. This is due to the age limitations we imposed on our sample and to the small membership of many of these existing clubs. Our effort to obtain the list proved worthwhile since it enabled us to recognize obscure activities as legitimate if respondents did name them.

Our final list consisted of ten main types of voluntary

associations: church-related groups (that is, voluntary associations associated with churches); regular lodges; mutual-aid lodges; veterans' associations; parent-teachers associations; political clubs; professional, business, and service groups; sports and athletics clubs; social groups, such as dancing or card clubs; and Negro-rights organizations. A residual category ("any other") was included in the schedule, but proved unnecessary in the analysis because every organization could be included in the above set.

A dichotomous grouping of the ten organization types can be used to examine the instrumental-expressive typology. For this research, expressive voluntary associations will consist of the following categories from our more concrete typology: regular lodges, church-related, veterans', sports, and social clubs. The instrumental category includes the remaining ones: mutual-aid lodges, PTA, local political, professional, and Negro-rights groups. The allocation of the voluntary association types to these categories was made on the basis of our estimate of the public function of the organization, as mentioned previously. There is little doubt about the classification of most of them, and the mixed category of instrumental-expressive would apply only situationally and occasionally to regular lodges, mutual-aid lodges, and Negro-rights groups. In fact, we are inclined to claim that the institutionalized procedures for organizational formation in the Negro community tend to the sect-like rather than the church-like mode. From this we would deduce that there would be fewer mixed-category organizations in Negro than in white communities. The Gordon and Babchuk typology is not oriented to such distinctions.

TAMPA'S NEGRO
VOLUNTARY ASSOCIATIONS

In our attempts to place membership in voluntary associations in perspective, Tampa's newness as a metropolis looms large. Organizations do not exist in a vacuum—each community shapes and molds its voluntary associations in its own way. Let us, therefore, describe some of the more important features of the research city, which add meaning to the descriptions of organizations themselves.

Tampa is a medium-size city that shares its metropolitan features with adjacent St. Petersburg. It has a variety of manufacturing, service, and commercial activity, along with a substantial seaport. Population growth has been very recent.

This growth, largely since World War II, occurred in an old, small, fairly isolated town. The result is that the residential areas tend toward low housing density. Tampa sprawls. There are very few multiple-unit dwellings in the old sections of the city, which have predominantly Negro occupancy. Moreover, these older areas often were inhabited by Spanish and Italian speaking populations, each of which emphasized single-family dwellings. Consequently, the older areas in which Negroes reside are composed largely of single-family frame houses.

There is no Negro upper-class residential area and only very small distinctly middle-class areas. There are six Negro residential areas. These areas are not close together. Several of the smaller ones are too far apart for normal daily interaction.

Tampa is in many respects a diversified ethnic community. In addition to Negroes, there are substantial populations of Italian and Spanish (largely "old" and "new" Cuban) and a number of other smaller ethnic populations. To some extent these ethnic populations have taken up distinctive occupations, (for example, Cuban cigar-makers) as well as distinctive residential locations. As usual the possible work choices for Negroes have been few, mainly in the manual occupations. However, these have tended to be in diversified and small employment settings. There are no massive corporations to provide a clear and powerful basis for linkage of sustenance organizations to the political and social life of the community.

All of this points to a diffused, fragmented, isolated, and dispersed set of groups in Tampa, among Negroes as well as among whites, and between both. As each type of voluntary association is examined, these features will be highlighted where appropriate.

Church-Related Organizations

The extensive development of churches among Negroes is paralleled by a similar proliferation of church-related organizations.[5] We expected to find that these organizations would be numerous because of the institutionalized limits imposed on Negroes' ability to freely form other, nonchurch organizations when and where they pleased—a limit not found in equal degree among whites, who can and do innovate without the restrictions of race. The church has had great salience for Negroes, but not only because slaveowners and then reconstruction white leaders felt religion was good for Negroes, or because Negroes are naturally religious. Neither is the prevalence of churches explained by a segregated society. The main reason is that the church was an institutionalized organization that Negroes themselves controlled. It had its synthesis in the heart of the Negro community, and therefore adapted its functions to a variety of needs that were unique there and that other, nonchurch associations met among whites. This stress toward ubiquity and utility was always in tension with the tendency of the Negro church toward other-worldly religion and its orientation to noninvolvement with everyday matters. There was also a tension between the church and its many organizations along sacred-profane lines.

This functional uniqueness of the church in Negro communities has also meant that churches and their clergy are power centers, perhaps more so than in non-Negro communities (with due account for the relative prominence of Protestantism among Negroes) and therefore that church-related voluntary associations are similarly salient. It may also be true that the prominence of Protestantism among Negroes is not only due to the Protestantism of slaveholders, but because of the more ready adaptability of Protestant types of organization to power synthesis in the Negro community. Consistent with this is our finding of black Catholicism as an upper-class religion, matching the whiteward mobility of disengaged Negro elites.

Even when we narrowly defined church-related as those voluntary associations that had a name, an independent governing apparatus, and independent meetings or events (thus excluding committees and operating divisions of the church itself), and that functioned in the community essentially as did other voluntary associations, we were surprised at the number of church-related associations. For the 80 churches with predominantly Negro membership in the research area (about one for every 800 Negroes), African Methodist Episcopal churches had 2.6 church-related associations per church, 24 Baptist churches had 2.7 per church, Missionary Baptist had 2.9, and Primitive Baptist had 3.0, as revealed by reported activities in the newspapers over a sample period of 6 months.[6]

Here are some samples of the kinds of organizations that we found in the research area.[7] Allen Temple A.M.E. Choir Number Two, Apostolic Church of Jesus of Palm Alley Mission Number Two, Bethel Baptist Junior Ushers, Evening Star Gospel Singers, Faith Temple Usher Union Number Three, Grace Mary Baptist Temperance Union, Greater Bethel Baptist Church Floral and Beautification Club, House of God Saints in Christ Baptist Young People's Union, Mount Pleasant Missionary Junior Women, New Mount Zion Missionary Baptist Calhoun Gospel Choir, New Salem Missionary Baptist Loyalty Club, Pleasant Chapel Willing Workers, St. John Missionary Baptist Deacon Board.

We found that 21 percent of our respondents belonged to a church-related voluntary association.

Regular Lodges

Many lodges found among Negroes are segregated versions of all-white organizations.[8] They bear familiar names—Masons, Elks, and the like—and have feminine counterparts. They tend to be less elegant than white lodges, and comparatively few are sufficiently established to boast a telephone. Eleven percent of our respondents belonged to regular lodges.

Mutual-Aid Lodges

The distinction between regular lodges and mutual-aid lodges is a matter of major functions. Regular lodges have a reputation of helping members and nonmembers, though they do not have this as a primary purpose. For some people they are identical. Thus, we asked a Negro professional if he would join the Masons, and he replied: "No, I can afford to buy insurance."

The most prominent mutual-aid lodges are the Grand Pallbearers Union and the Lily White Security Benefit Association. Each is a response to a particular need of the Negro community, which has a tragic history of inadequate security of person and fortune. Frazier's comment would apply accurately in Florida.

> Because of their precarious economic position in cities the free Negroes organized mutual-aid societies. These societies not only provided mutual aid, but encouraged saving and the accumulation of wealth. In a number of cities there were individual Negroes who engaged in money lending, using the wealth which they had accumulated as a barber or carpenter for capital.[9]

Negroes in Florida, as elsewhere, are poorly served by insurance companies and are often their victims rather than beneficiaries. Even where the insurance company is Negro controlled, it takes a form that is difficult for the uneducated Negro to understand—it involves conceptual abstractions that are foreign. The mutual-aid lodge is much more real to him: it is a merger of Christian indigenous cultural elements with practical solutions to the problem of financial security. The lodges achieve the synthesis of religion and economy that the churches cannot accomplish.

There is a further advantage in the lodge form of financial security—it can provide for an interest in gambling without the difficulty of a head-on conflict with the churchly opposition to sin. The lodge does this by allowing the distribution of death benefits to take the form of a payoff to the beneficiary of a successful bet that he would survive the insured. The payoff involves dividing the pot yearly, rather than a reliance on actuarial procedures calculated to bring a predictable fixed return. In many ways the mutual-aid lodge prospers because it is an indigenous form of voluntary association, responsive to community values and responsible to its members.

In addition to their financial aspects, the lodges have social events, a variety of meetings, and local chapter activities. The Lily White organization, in cooperation with the Longshoremen's Union, is active in public housing development. It provides health care and exerts leadership in many aspects of community affairs.

Burial societies are likewise an indigenous Negro-developed mechanism for the provision of services denied them by segregation practices. Frazier notes the simultaneous development of burial societies and lodges during the reconstruction era.[10]

Eight percent of our respondents reported that they belonged to a mutual-aid lodge.

Veterans' Groups

Veterans' voluntary associations are not prominent among Negroes.[11] Discrimination in national veterans' groups reflects the practices in the armed forces themselves, which only in recent years have begun to change. Veterans' organizations do not hold the prominent place in Negro communities that they do among whites, and Negro veterans' organizations rarely get publicity in the community newspapers. On the other hand, men in military service are prominently featured in news stories and their accomplishments are heralded.

Less then 2 percent of our respondents reported that they belonged to a veterans' organization.

Parent-Teacher Associations

The PTA, unlike the veterans' associations, is perhaps as prominent in the Negro communities of the research areas as in white ones. It may be that the greater proportion of less-educated parents among Negroes and the prevalence of aged and crowded schools in Negro residential areas leads to numerous membership problems for the Negro PTA. In the past, segregated schools meant monoracial PTAs. PTAs are still essentially monoracial, and in many areas Negro PTAs are oriented toward social action favoring civil rights and antipoverty programs.

Twelve percent of our respondents reported that they belonged to a PTA.

Political Voluntary Associations

The variety and range of political activity in any community is not easily metered by counting the number of political clubs or membership in them, since political activity may originate in a variety of places and typically is carried out by interested individuals through the instrumentality of other groups. Political activity in Negro communities in the research city is dominated by white politicians with whom Negro leaders work to get benefits for their neighborhoods (and for themselves). Despite intense and successful drives for voter registration in recent years, Negroes have, with minor exceptions, only increased the size of the electorate that chooses among white candidates. Since city officials

are all elected at large, Negroes cannot take advantage
of their concentration in certain areas (100 percent by district, 17 percent of the city population) to elect black representation from their areas. Indeed, the actual situation seems
to be that predominantly Negro districts typically vote solidly
for old-style southern white political candidates, and not for
liberals or reformers. Despite increasing Negro pressure on
officials and some responsiveness from the halls of power,
Negro politics appears dormant. In most cases it is still the
futile action of a very few people. In such a situation, Negro
political clubs would not be expected, and indeed we found
very few respondents (about 1 percent) who claimed participation.

In our discussion of church groups, we mentioned the
stress on churches to serve as substitute power centers in
Negro communities. The power issue arose also in conjunction with the local antipoverty programs in Negro communities, which seemed for a time to offer a new source
of political power to the Negro masses, bypassing political
structures that comprehensively restricted them. The surge
of hope in the Negro groups in the research area was soon
replaced by cynicism, as white-dominated political power was
asserted in new ways through control of the governing
apparatus of poverty programs and related institutional arrangements. For example, the governing council of city
poverty programs persistently met during the day, following
the convenience of white businessmen and Negro professionals, when most Negro and poor white workers could
not attend. In general, the poverty programs apparently
offered a source of pluralism and associational participation
to Negro masses, but in a way which could not fructify. Like

the political clubs and other voluntaristic sources of participation in society, they soon fell back into the old segregated way of life.

We conclude that political-club and antipoverty program participation have much in common—they illustrate the difficulties that Negroes encounter when they make an effort to be participants in society. One result is very little political associational activity.

Professional, Business, and Service Groups

In both chapters 1 and 2 we dealt extensively with the nature of the connection between work and voluntary associations of professionals and business people. Our task here is to present concrete detail and explanation about the professional, business, and service voluntary associations to which the Negroes belong.

To describe the voluntary associations of Negro professionals is largely to describe organizations of, by, and for whites.[12] To describe Negro business associations is also largely futile; there are not many Negro businessmen, there is not much Negro business, and therefore we see a gap in the organizational structure of the Negro community that sharply affects Negroes' ability to get what they want when they want it.

Membership in the professional category is comprised of a substantial membership in teachers' organizations and only a few others. The bulk consists of organizations that match the main categories of the teacher's professional identity; the county teachers' associations, the classroom teachers' groups, the education association, the teaching specialty associations, and scholarly societies.[13]

Five percent of our total respondents report membership in a professional or business voluntary association.

Sports and Athletic Clubs

Of the range of leisure activities found in the Negro communities, we have selected only those that take voluntary associational form. By this selection we eliminate from consideration those leisure activities for youth that are sponsored by schools as an integral part of their programs, supervised activities of the city recreation service, various commercial ventures, and casual sports activities. Once again, the findings are meager. Insofar as such activities require use of buildings and grounds, Negroes are disadvantaged by both poverty and segregation. Although the separate but equal ideology was nominally followed in Tampa for generations, like everywhere, the truth was that Negroes were effectively excluded from participation in a considerable proportion of the sports readily available to whites and, related integrally to this, from social organizations associated with them.

We encountered no Negroes who claimed membership in sports voluntary associations that required unrestricted access to the costly facilities associated with individual performance, such as golf, swimming, and the racquet sports. Negroes tend, rather, to a high rate of participation in sports such as football and basketball, which are parts of programs of large urban high schools. In these sports, participation is via nonvoluntary associations such as schools, or in leisure time recreation leagues, which are typically segregated. Negroes usually are not found in individual performance sports because, in addition to being victims of social discrimination, Negroes are members of a mass society in which mass participation is institutionalized. Insofar as Negroes participate in white-dominated team sports sponsored by the recreation department or city wide leagues, they are accepted on teams that adequately regulate social relations of players. This formal regulation ceases at the end of the contest, typically giving way to informal exclusion. Negroes are welcomed as performers, not as persons.[14]

Individual performance sports, however, involve a much greater orientation to regulation by means of informal relations off the field of play, which depends in turn on a general social environment that is a web of relationships of status equals. Therefore, the social-club element is of basic significance in tennis, golf, and the like, while there is little need for a club in football outside of the team itself. This distinction between social organization of the sport and social organization of the team is crucial. We think it is of equal importance to the element of social class or economic requirements of the sport, which has so often been stressed.

Social Voluntary Associations

Although we might expect the obvious segregation of social relations to limit Negro participation in sports voluntary associations, there is no reason to expect small clubs and organizations to be limited in a similar fashion. Clubs for parties, conversation, dancing, gambling, and so on are easily formed and readily adapted to local interests. It is therefore not surprising to find a specific style of voluntary association formation for purely social reasons institutionalized among the young and matched by adult clubs.[15] The following is a selected list of representative social organizations of the research city: The Ebonair, Jolly Few, Rosettes, Friendly Fifteen, Leisure Hour, Trojans, Fiesta, Paradise, Even Better, La Charm, Falcon, Shirelles, Blue Dahlia, Idle Hour, Blue Swan, Widows, Wee Bankers, Entre Nous, Skycaps, Our Own, La Sans Souci, Cha Cha Cha, Las Amegias [*sic*], Working Women's, Pearly Gates, La Paris. The clubs average slightly more than ten members each. Many of them operate on an annual basis, with major social events just before Christmas, followed by division of the remaining funds and dissolution of the club leading to a new start in January.[16]

We have not found any substantial study of social groups of this sort in the sociological literature since the national work of Myrdal and the Chicago study of Drake and Cayton more than twenty years ago.[17] Our comments on the organizations in the research city are therefore without a comparative base. We suggest the following interpretation.

Negro communities are deficient in power. Generally they lack the tall status structure typical of white communities of similar size. We have shown this in a variety of examples: the lack of political machinery, the lack of associational strength among businessmen (associational, not merely voluntary associational), deficits in education, lack of businesses in the central business district, and so on. Moreover, they usually lack a stable upper class. Among whites, voluntary associations closely parallel the power structure and assist in the consolidation of power. The status compression of the Negro community is responsible for deficits in reliable means of exhibition, declaration, and cashing-in of prestige. One way out in such situations is to seek to substitute esteem for prestige, but even the basis for creation of esteem becomes uncertain. Under such circumstances, the need for prestige-conferring organizations is crucial, precisely when their effectiveness is in doubt. Ironically the management of both impression and depression become crucial, simultaneously. Negroes become insecure about prestige and rely on usurpation of honor, in the absence of secure claims to power. There is a burden on the voluntary association and the church in Negro communities: they must be the vehicles of prestige conferral to a larger degree than their ability allows. Thus we would expect the search for prestige to be accompanied by high degrees of elaboration, emphasis on display, and ultimately the discovery of the unstable nature of such forms of organization. The taller the status structure, the more stable the prestige-conferring organizations.

This process of institutionalization of organization formation is recognized and there are reactions to it. Ministers in the research area, for example, speak frequently of poor people who do not want to attend church because their clothing is shabby. Some ministers deal with this problem by having "old clothes days" at church, probably unsuccessfully. (Children are frequently dressed neatly and formally at church, perhaps more so than in white churches in the same area, by our impression.) Behind it all is the deeply ingrained assumption of Negroes themselves that what they do will not be of much consequence.

The community newspaper gives extensive coverage to social events. Pictures from parties frequently cover several pages and may appear in several consecutive issues.[18]

From the foregoing discussion and from the works cited we would expect a high rate of membership in clubs.

We found, however, that only 4 percent of our respondents claimed membership in a social organization. Our concentrated attention to sampling and to the methodology of asking questions leads us to state this finding with a high degree of confidence. It seems necessary, then, to explain the belief that Negroes are greatly involved in social events when the evidence is contrary.

Several sources of this belief can be examined with data at hand. One is the fact that some people belong to many clubs. A second is the small size of the clubs—the finding by Drake and Cayton of thousands of clubs in Chicago does not prove that there are many people in clubs, but only that there are many clubs. And further, if we include the frequent refounding of clubs, it is quite likely that many clubs were counted more than once by Drake and Cayton. The newspapers lend credence to the belief that there is a great deal of social activity among prestigious Negroes and Negroes in general. A scientific sample returns a different verdict: there is a lot of display and a lot of noise, but the masses do not participate very much in social-club organizations. The explanation proposed at the start of this section must then be modified by our findings: there is indeed much striving for display and attempt at cashing-in of prestige, but the masses of Negroes do not participate in such modes of voluntary associations. They often utilize less formal media of social life to meet their needs.

Insights into contemporary Negro life by such writers as Keil and Liebow would seem to support such a conclusion: the "Urban Blues" is a phenomenon of virtuoso individual performance with a mass following.[19] It is exemplary charisma, not voluntary association, that unites large numbers of Negroes and James Brown or Otis Redding, not Whitney Young or Roy Wilkins, who embody their ideals.

Negro-Rights Organizations

This category includes only those organizations whose sole purpose is some aspect of racial advance or progress and excludes those having only subsidiary civil-rights activities. The most prominent of these locally is the National Association for the Advancement of Colored People.[20] The National Urban League has a local branch.[21] There have been several smaller social action groups without national affiliation, but none of them gained prominence. The Council on Human Relations, an interracial group affiliated with the Southern Regional Council, has been erratically active. Some churches have had social action groups with occasional involvement in race relations. Strictly speaking, the Black Muslims are a church and not a voluntary association, and cannot be counted here, although their militance is well known locally.[22] The National Conference of Christians and Jews has a local chapter with interracial membership.

The Southern Christian Leadership Conference was not well known locally, though its president, Martin Luther King, Jr., was widely esteemed.[23] The Congress of Racial Equality[24] and the Student Nonviolent Coordinating Committee[25] were active and controversial in the South at the time of data gathering, but neither had active local branches. In general, militant organizations have not had strong support locally, in spite of the existence of long-standing grievances in the Negro community. This issue will be dealt with more comprehensively when we take up the effect on voluntary associations of the 1967 Tampa riot.

Eleven percent of our respondents claimed membership in one or more Negro-rights groups.

In our examination of the ten kinds of voluntary associations and explanation of their features, we often found it necessary to qualify the apparent meaning of their attributes. A simple count of associations or report of membership frequency by no means tells us all we want to know. We now turn from the organizational to the membership perspective on voluntary associations: the distribution of memberships in various combinations and concentrations, in the kinds of organizations, and in multiple organizations of the same kind.

PATTERNS OF MEMBERSHIP: THE TEN TYPES

Membership Totals

In this section we are concerned both with the person as actor and with his membership in the organization. Sometimes these are simply reciprocal, as when a person belongs to only one organization. At other times, a more formal analysis is required; as, for example, when we consider the church-related organizations that have a high proportion of members who belong to two or more of this type as well as to other types.

The gross percentage membership in each type has been presented above, with the description of each type.

We found that the type of voluntary association to which respondents most often belonged was one related to a church (frequently but not necessarily including membership in the church). One-fifth of all respondents belonged to a church-related association. Approximately one-tenth of all respondents belonged to a PTA, and when we consider the 20-60 age limit of our sample, this voluntary association looms as one of great importance for the age segment involved. A smaller percentage of respondents belonged to the lodges, social, professional, sports, and Negro-rights types, and tied for last were veterans and political groups, which had a membership of about 1 percent each.

The frequent membership in church-related and PTA types is perhaps partially explained by the easy accessibility of these groups to potential members. Not only is membership by virtually everyone encouraged, but also they are decentralized and attached to and supported by other groups (churches and schools) that have permanent staffs, accessible facilities, and public approval or mandate.

Negro-rights organizations are another matter. Although they typically have open membership, many are centralized, which serves to make attendance and even joining more difficult than, say, the dispersed and accessible PTAs. Perhaps they enjoy an appeal as wide as the PTA by virtue of their community-serving function; they do typically attempt to speak for the total Negro community in a way that church-related and PTA types do not or cannot. The NAACP is perhaps the single, centralized unit expressing the interests of the total Negro community. This suggests that the use of voluntary associations alone to identify a pluralistic society is perhaps too gross: we may wish to distinguish between decentralized, local pluralism and the pluralism reflected by units that integrate the total community. On the other hand, regular and mutual-aid lodges each also claim about one-tenth of the research population as members.

Each of the remaining voluntary association types has only a small membership among the respondents. One way of emphasizing this is to point out that if there were no overlap in membership, altogether these types would command a membership only about equivalent to the members of the PTA alone.

Multiple Membership

In chapter 2 we noted the several characteristics of the multiple joiner—the pluralist man. In this section, we rejoin that issue from another perspective. What mix of organizations do joiners join? The issue is an important one that, strangely, has not been studied. If pluralists join many organizations of the same kind, the societal results would be different than if they joined one of each of several kinds. Multiple membership in one kind we may term *intensivity*, and multiple membership spanning more than one kind, *extensivity*. Intensivity is an aspect of community integration. Of course the formal relations of organizations themselves, or their consensus on values regardless of their structural connections, also are basic aspects of these same phenomena, and we must stress that intensivity and extensivity are only some aspects of cleavage and integration. Intensivity is not the same as *specialization*, which refers to exclusive participation in one organization. In addition, there is reason to assume that for some persons multiple membership serves not as a means to community integration, but as a way of coping with cross-pressures resulting from conflicting demands of contradictory statuses, by dealing with them in separate times and places and with different people.

Our discussion in chapter 1 of types of work and our description in this chapter of types of organizations lead us to some predictions about intensivity and extensivity. The organizations professionals join might frequently be characterized by intensivity and there is no apparent reason to assume that intensivity would be the consequence of work-related variables among low blue-collar workers. In addition, since so many pluralists are white-collar, we predict that intensivity is likely to characterize the pluralists more often than extensivity.

Obviously, factors other than social relations of work will affect the distribution of things that pluralists join. Among these would be personal needs for variety and leisure, which are causally remote from our research variables. We will not, therefore, attempt any formal theory of distribution patterns of multiple memberships, but we can present the data and offer interpretation of findings.

Intensivity is measured by the relative number of respondents belonging to at least one organization of a given type who belong to more than one of that type (regardless of whether they have other memberships). That is, we ask only of those who belong, do they belong to more than one of that type. The data is presented in Table 9. Professional, business and service, and church-related voluntary associations clearly have far more multiple membership than do other types. Put another way, those who join one of type A are more likely to join at least one more of type A than those who join one of type B are to join a second of type B.

TABLE 9

INTENSIVITY OF MULTIPLE MEMBERSHIP
IN TEN TYPES OF VOLUNTARY ASSOCIATIONS

	(1) Percent of total sample with memberships in	(2) Percent of those belonging who belong to more of type	(3) Percent of total sample belonging to 2 or more of each type
Church-related (E)[a]	21	26	6
Regular lodges (E)	11	8	1
Mutual-aid lodges (I)[b]	8	2	1
Veterans (E)	2	—	—
PTA (I)	12	2	1
Political (I)	1	11	1
Professional, business, service (I)	5	39	2
Sports (E)	2	11	1
Social clubs (E)	4	7	1
Negro-rights (I)	11	7	1

[a] E = Expressive.
[b] I = Instrumental.

The explanation may be that teachers are more likely to belong to two or more PTAs (as parents and teachers) and professional business and service associations.

Multiple membership varies among other types of voluntary associations from none (for veterans' voluntary associations) to 11 percent among political and sports types. Both of these, however, have such small membership as to make it unwise to interpret these remaining differences.

The proportion of the total sample who belong to two or more voluntary associations of a given type is small. The single voluntary association type that commands the greatest multiple membership (6 percent of the total sample) is the church-related. This finding must be viewed with caution, since we assumed that church-related voluntary associations are separate or autonomous, and not just committees or extensions of church administration. For other organizations, such as lodges, we did not delineate any lodge-related groups. There is a possibility that we have simply not asked the right questions of respondents.

The apparent predominance of church-related intensivity has some bearing on a question of long standing in Negro communities: the conflict between the demands of religion and secular life. Insofar as voluntary associational life is an indicator, church and profession are the two main organizational competitors for the time and loyalty of Negroes, but the low overall rates of type specialization suggest that the schism is on the ideological level, and does not involve a large number of people.

The low proportion of extensivity may be inferred from the extreme irregularity of column 2 in Table 9. A regular distribution would indicate a tendency to diffusion of participation in accordance with personal interest.

The frequency of participation in church-related voluntary associations is, of course, closely related to the high rate of church membership in the community. We can further study the community integrative function of religious participation by examining variations in multiple membership as to types of voluntary associations by church and nonchurch categories. We find from the data that respondents who belong to a church are more likely to belong to a church-related group (obviously), both kinds of lodges, PTA, professional, or Negro-rights groups, but are not more likely to join veterans', political, sports, or social clubs.

When we analyze the church membership of those who belong to more than one organization of one kind, we find that church membership is positively correlated with intensivity in both kinds of lodges, church-related, PTA, professional, and Negro-rights groups as before, but also for all the other kinds of voluntary associations for which there is any appreciable number of members.

Because there is no organization other than the church that enrolls a majority of the population, the same kind of analysis cannot be made of the integrative potential of other kinds of organizations. We do not, however, automatically assume the integrative value of churches because church members are pluralists—the frequent disputes between churches and their inability to unite on crucial values would make this too strong a conclusion. In fact, some evidence of the nonfunctionality of church membership can be assumed from examination of attendance at voluntary association meetings. Attendance at meetings is higher among church members than nonchurch members, in church-related, veterans', PTA, professional, and service groups, but not higher or even lower for church members who belong to lodges or Negro-rights organizations. Church membership apparently does not affect attendance in sports, political, or social groups. The reason for these findings is not readily apparent, but it is likely that practical matters such as frequency of meetings and time conflicts are to be considered. Certainly no simple explanation of value conflict along sacred/profane lines can be accepted, since there seems to be little such difference among these organizations in community life, nor can the claim be made that social or sports clubs keep people from joining a church.

The obvious difference in the patterns of variation in attendance and membership suggests further examination of attendance as a source of explanation of voluntary association life.

Membership, Attendance, Leadership

All studies show that attendance is more rare than claimed membership. Our data, by type of voluntary association, affirm this, but there is also variation in the ratio of attendance to membership by types of association. Over 90 percent of all members claim they have attended at least one meeting during the last year, except for those who belong to mutual-aid lodges, veterans', PTA, and Negro-rights voluntary associations. One possible interpretation is that those voluntary associations that have relatively few members who attend are often joined for prestige (perhaps the reverse, considered causally) or for benefits that may accrue regardless of participation (such associations may also tend to be larger and oligarchic).[26]

In chapter 1 we reasoned that we could expect a higher ratio of participation to membership among expressive than among instrumental voluntary associations. That collateral hypothesis can be tested here. There is some support for it. Among the ten types of voluntary associations the median falls between 90 and 91 percent in the attendance-to-membership ratio. Four of the five expressive type associations are above the median, and four of the five instrumental types are below. Assuming the independence of membership in these types, Fisher's Exact Test reveals statistical significance at the .05 level.

In Table 10 some of the combinations of belonging,

TABLE 10

MEMBERSHIP, ATTENDANCE, AND OFFICE-HOLDING
IN TEN TYPES OF VOLUNTARY ASSOCIATIONS

PERCENTS	TYPES OF VOLUNTARY ASSOCIATIONS[a]									
	1	2	3	4	5	6	7	8	9	10
(1) Belonging	21	11	8	2	12	1	5	2	4	11
(2) Attendance of those who belong	97	91	86	75	82	100	90	95	98	69
(3) Attendance of those who belong to 2 or more of type	98	100	100	—	67	100	100	100	100	100
(4) Officeholders among those who belong	32	19	11	8	3	11	14	26	38	3
(5) Officeholders among those who belong to 1 of type	24	20	11	8	3	13	10	24	38	2

TABLE 10 (Continued)

PERCENTS	TYPES OF VOLUNTARY ASSOCIATIONS[a]									
	1	2	3	4	5	6	7	8	9	10
(6) Officeholders among those who belong to 2 or more of type	57	11	50	—	—	—	21	50	33	25
(7) Attendance and officers who belong to only 1 organization	23	18	11	8	2	13	10	24	38	2
(8) Attendance and officers who belong to 2 or more organizations	55	11	50	—	—	—	21	50	33	25

[a] Types of organizations: 1 = church-related, 2 = regular lodges, 3 = mutual-aid lodges, 4 = veterans, 5 = PTA, 6 = political, 7 = professional, business and service, 8 = sports, 9 = social clubs, 10 = Negro-rights.

attending, and holding office can be seen. Row 1 is reproduced from Table 9. The percent attending who belong
is essentially the same as the percent attending who belong
to only one of the type, and so the latter has been omitted.

Those who belong to two or more voluntary associations of a given type are equally likely, or more likely, to
attend each than are those who belong to just one of a given
type, with the exception of the PTA. It is probably the case
that respondents with two or more PTA memberships are
likely to be teachers and/or parents with children in different
schools (Tampa has junior high schools as well as primary
schools and high schools). A teacher who also has three
children each three years apart in age may be eligible for
and expected to show an interest in three or perhaps four
PTAs, and probably at least one professional association.
Although Negro teachers are often correctly acclaimed as
community leaders, we suggest that some of them unknow-
ingly (and perhaps unwillingly) "skid upward" into leadership.[27] At any rate, these data seem to indicate that membership in the PTA more often is nominal—or coerced—than
membership in other types of voluntary associations. The
data on the other types indicate that multiple membership
is accompanied by greater participation and perhaps this
means that persons who belong to more than one group of
a given type do so because they are interested in the voluntary association's activities. It may also be true that membership in more than one of a type of voluntary association
simply represents the existence of more opportunities, and
pressure, to participate.

In chapter 1 we discussed the problem of phasing of
work and the diurnal cycle of community life, which limits

membership for certain people. About 20 percent of those who have jobs work other than "only the day shift," and are thus 120° or some other degree out of phase with dominant community patterns. The data, however, are to be unreliable, since low blue-collar workers may shift unpredictably from one type of work to another. To the extent that unemployment is erratic among the low blue-collar, we underestimate the amount of phase segregation that such workers can expect to experience. The 20 percent finding is fairly consistent among occupations, although it is slightly higher for the white-collar workers. However, not many Negroes work only night or evening shifts. Rather, swing shifts and multiple job holding account for one-half or more of those who confront some form of phase-induced restriction in their activities. We did not expect white-collar workers to be similar to blue-collar workers as to phase segregation, because white-collar workers generally have better control over hours of work or speak favorably of their hours. It must be assumed that here the meaning of out-of-phase work is not the same, so far as ability to control one's own time is concerned, and that white-collar workers generally have more discretionary time without penalty than blue-collar, even though for the set the proportions of phase deviance are similar. Tables 39 and 40, Appendix B, contain compilations relevant to these issues.

The chance visitor to downtown Tampa at dawn on Sunday may see an unexpected sight. Near deserted metropolitan churches are large groups of Negro men, queued up outside the Longshoremen's Union headquarters, waiting for another day of work. Nearby is the bus depot, where more Negro men carry out their occasional morning duties. Negro cabdrivers wait outside hotels for fares. There are whites, too, but Sunday dawn is an hour of Negro blue-collar work, out of phase diurnally and weekly.

Phasing probably effects attendance primarily and membership derivatively. Analogously, we must consider the relative effect of other phasing cycles of community life on membership and attendance. The weekly cycle traditionally alternates between religious and profane affairs. Religious groups claim Sunday, which is structured traditionally and reinforced by various shades of blue laws. We would assume that the large proportion of Negroes in service occupations often leads to Sunday employment and a corresponding weakening of their ties to religious groups.

On the other hand, the traditions regarding use of Saturday and Sunday have a distinct effect on the prominence of religious organizations in all communities. The relatively lower proportion among Negroes of those who have Sundays free may be a factor in the structure of their participation in religious organizations. But of course, many who have free time do not use it for community voluntary association life.

Another perspective on voluntary associations concerns the percentage of members who are officers. There are substantial differences among organizations. Approximately one-third of the members of at least one church-related or social club voluntary association claim officerships of some type. This finding involves some redundancy: the qualification for joining some groups (e.g., Deacon's Board) is that one be an officer of another group. Regular lodges and sports groups rank next (with one-fifth to one-fourth officers), followed by professional, business and service, and mutual-aid lodges. Veterans', PTA, political, and Negro-rights have very small officer-to-member ratios.

Certain features of the community style of institutionalization of group formation explain these findings. The practice of reorganizing social clubs on a yearly basis means that organizing activity is a constant feature of club life, and perhaps even a latent purpose of the club. This organizing process in small groups is also true of sports voluntary associations. At the other extreme are those kinds that have charters or mandates from national or state organizations, which control finances, specify the offices and procedures, and provide for continuity and stability by various means, including a staff, central bureaucracy, or traditional leadership. Such groups can become quite large and still have small cadres of officerships that often become oligarchies. The annual organizations are constantly engaged in dealing with the interrelations of people, jobs, activities, offices, and statuses. The problem of the small organization is to fit the many aspects together and survive, while the problem of the large, permanent organization is fitting people to established offices and statuses and motivating performance. In this permanent category are the veterans', PTA, political, and the national (but not local) Negro-rights organizations.

This reasoning does not explain the relatively high proportion of officers in regular lodges. If lodges are generally losing membership, as has often been claimed, we might expect to find numerous residual traditional offices, relatively many older members who hold them, low attendance, and a diminishing membership gradually rising in average age. We do not have sufficient information to substantiate this idea.

The four kinds of organizations that have the lowest attendance figures, mutual-aid lodges, veterans', PTA, and Negro-rights, also have small proportions of officers. The phenomena of leadership, high attendance, and multiple belonging in the same person, on the other hand, is most pronounced in the mutual-aid lodges, church-related, and sports groups, followed closely by social clubs. With the exception of the lodge, these feature small size and frequent reformation.

PATTERNS OF MEMBERSHIP AND ATTENDANCE: EXPRESSIVE AND INSTRUMENTAL ORGANIZATIONS

In this chapter we have considered concrete voluntary associations themselves, the patterns of membership of individuals in them and, from the perspective of the organization, the distribution of memberships. We turn now to the second classification of organizations, that of expressive versus instrumental. This raises new questions of importance about all three approaches. This is an abstract conceptualization of the social characteristics of voluntary associations; intensivity versus extensivity is an abstract classification of an individual's memberships.

Unfortunately, the need to distinguish different levels of analysis cannot be accompanied by a corresponding adequacy of data. To consider the expressive versus instrumental category thoroughly would involve research methods suitable to the consideration of organizations as actors in a complex of social systems. Our decision to proceed by means of survey research precludes this kind of investigation. We are limited to data obtained from respondents and inference from their statements about the organizational level of behavior, and we should not extrapolate beyond those data. This section, therefore, must play a minor part in our reasoning about community life, and can be treated succinctly.

The expressive organizations (more precisely, those that we have called expressive) are the regular lodges, church-related, veterans', sports, and social clubs. The instrumental are the mutual-aid lodges, PTA, political, professional, and Negro-rights groups. The distribution of membership in terms of these categories can be seen by reference to Table 9. The percentages in column 1 cannot be summed because the figures involve membership in categories, and some people belong to more than one group within a category or to more than one category.

It can be readily seen, however, that church-related (expressive) lead in proportion of membership, while the total number of memberships (not total people) is divided almost equally between expressive and instrumental.

Intensivity, as indicated in column 2 of Table 9, is concentrated in an instrumental organization type, the professional, business and service, with an expressive organization, the church-related, in second place. Trailing these two leaders, the remainder are relatively evenly distributed.

Column 3 of Table 9, unlike column 1, can be summed for memberships. It shows that the percentage of the research population who belong to two or more of a kind tend to do so more often in expressive than instrumental organizations by about half. Thus, about 9 percent of all respondents belong to two or more expressive associations of a given type, whereas 6 percent of all respondents belong to two or more instrumental associations of a given type.

When attendance patterns are analyzed for expressive

and instrumental orientations (see Table 10), we find that attendance is generally more frequent in the expressive than the instrumental type. Intensivity of membership is associated with an increase in attendance for all types except the PTA, which drops sharply with multiple membership.[28]

The most severe demands for leadership in a particular type of organization are indicated by the proportion who belong to two or more of a given kind and attend and hold office. The proportion attending and holding office for this augmented measure of intensivity is highest in the church-related, and is in general more frequent in expressive than instrumental organizations. The greatest amounts of intensivity, leadership, and organizational loyalty in the Negro community are found in the expressive church-related, sports, and social clubs, rather than in the professional organizations (which, we have claimed, tend to be white-controlled) or Negro-rights organizations, which meet infrequently and apparently command only a nominal recognition, rather than active involvement. We shall encounter this issue again when we examine the impact of a major riot on Negroes' attitudes to their organizations. However, next we must examine more thoroughly the correlates of occupational status and the social conditions of employment on kind of joining.

NOTES

1. This distinction is to be made with caution, since the church in America has been subjected to many of the same social forces that led to the prominence of secular voluntary

associations. In the United States the sect has often taken an exploratory form in the search for religious purity; as a consequence, it has many of the characteristics we delineated for voluntary associations. The sect is the quintessence of the voluntary religious association; it stresses the similarity of members, who gain access only upon proof of qualification (typically as adults, and thus nonascriptive) and specificity of goals. Attempts to classify religious organizations typically have to add distinctions to dichotomies such as church and sect, which suggest that there may be a variety of degrees of voluntarism in religious as well as nonreligious organizations. The classical treatment of the distinction between sect and church is that of Ernst Troeltsch, *Social Teachings of the Christian Churches.* A more recent analysis with an attempt at classification of sects into four types is found in the work of Bryon Wilson, "An Analysis of Sect Development," *American Sociological Review* 24: 3–15.

2. C. Wayne Gordon and Nicholas Babchuk, "A Typology of Voluntary Associations," *American Sociological Review* 24: 22–29.

3. Parsons terms a collectivity in which expressive interests are primarily a "gemeinschaft," and one in which instrumental interests are the principal ones an "organization." To the extent that each is formal, they are also "associations" (Talcott Parsons, *The Social System,* p. 100). Parsons' original formulation has not always been strictly observed by those who apply the terms to voluntary associations.

4. In *The Joiners,* Hausknecht presents a summary of research findings regarding types of Negro membership. There is no reason to assume that the concrete types he uses have any relevance to the city in which our research took place. In fact, the data he cites seem to be based on the assumption that comparison of Negro and white rates of membership was necessary, and that Negro rates of membership are related to categories appropriate for white. Our research procedure differed somewhat from the sequence of presentation here, which has the appearance of operationism. Prior to the pilot studies, we had in mind

a rather general definition of voluntary associations, which is
evident in the kinds of distinctions made in chapter 1. The operational definitions followed from those distinctions. Our approach
has much in common with Andrew Billingsley's orientation to
the study of the Negro family *(Black Families in White
America);* we begin with general theory, and then examine Negro
behavior itself. This helps to avoid the value illusions that sometimes arise when research on Negroes has been done by whites.

5. E. Franklin Frazier, *The Negro Church in America,* is
the definitive work. Other sources on the Negro church contain more concrete detail than Frazier's, but are outdated and
are only suggestive for our purposes. We found Drake and
Cayton, and Myrdal, of general use in considering the relationship of church and church groups (St. Clair Drake and Horace
R. Cayton, *Black Metropolis;* Gunnar Myrdal, *An American
Dilemma).* Washington's *Black Religion* is more contemporary,
but less sociological (Joseph R. Washington, Jr., *Black Religion).*

6. We are grateful to Mr. Dewey Gaddis for his patient
service in gathering this information. He found evidence of some
bias in newspaper reporting of events, since some churches never
had any news coverage at all, yet independent observation demonstrated that the events did take place. The items reported are
probably accurate enough as to the existence of the associations,
but we cannot conclude anything decisive from this about their
importance or the actual frequency of their activities.

7. These are from newspaper items, and are not necessarily
associations named by respondents, who frequently used abbrevi-
ated popular names for them. The frequency with which they
belonged to such organizations was dependent on the respondent's
assertion that he participated in a church-related group, and
thus there is likely to be a bias toward church activities that are
more closely tied to the church than our abstract definition per-
mits. This subjectivity presents a problem that cannot be overlooked. We would argue that such named activities have the
function of voluntary associations in the communities, and although they come close to the ascriptive dimension at times,

they are distinct from the more specifically ascriptive phenomenon of belonging to a church to satisfy the community requirement to belong to *some church*. When it comes to comparison with other voluntary associations, we do not ask about subgroups of lodges, and the like.

8. The relation of Negro and white voluntary associations, and particularly lodges, was an important issue in Myrdal's classic study (*An American Dilemma*). He noted a lag phenomenon, with Negro organizations patterning themselves after white organizations, but with exaggerations. Whether this still exists, or if it ever did, is of little concern here. It should be noted, however, that in the research city there are both regular lodges that seem to have superficial similarities to white organizations, and mutual-aid lodges that are indigenous and unique. The classic work on fraternal associations is Charles W. Ferguson, *Fifty Million Brothers*.

9. E. Franklin Frazier, *Black Bourgeoisie*, p. 35.

10. Ibid., p. 39.

11. Neither Myrdal nor Drake and Cayton list a reference to Negro veterans' groups, and less encyclopedic works are similar.

12. Frazier has some scathing comments to make about Negro business and professional associations. In line with his thesis that the black bourgeoisie suffers from an inferiority complex, he sees their voluntary associations as essentially phony fronts or covers for their inferiority feeling. Negroes find segregated associations are necessary because they are excluded by whites, but the groups do not take professional life seriously and turn the associations into drinking clubs. The wounds Frazier inflicted brought roars of pain, as if it were betrayal of the race to expose the high-status members of society. We believe he made a sociological error more serious than the one for which he was castigated—he failed to put his statement in comparative perspective. The phoniness of Negro professional voluntary associations is matched if not exceeded by the similar behavior of many white organizations whose professional meetings follow the American norm of excessive drinking at conventions. Here,

if anywhere in American life, white and Negro behavior and norms are similar, not different. As a member of the American Sociological Society, Frazier should have known better. Frazier, *Black Bourgeoisie,* pp. 168–170.

13. It is relevant to ask whether or not these are voluntary, since advance and professional standing seem to require them. This bears on the meaning of membership, not its existence— and only the latter is of concern here. *Who's Who in Colored America* lists 79 honor societies and 94 professional societies to which Negroes belong. If we add Negro-rights associations, there are probably at least 200 national associations to which Negroes typically belong. Only a handful of these were mentioned by the respondents in this study. Most of them are "Greek letter" associations, and the fact that they are honor and professional societies indicates their white-collar nature. These include such mixed professional and business groups as the National Negro Business League and Sigma Delta Epsilon, a management professional association.

14. We are grateful to Mr. Robert Keeley for his insightful observations on recreation of Negroes in the research city, particularly as to modes of segregation in team sports.

15. In the second pilot study, which was mentioned at the start of this chapter, a comparison was made between the voluntary association membership rates of adults and their childrens' memberships in high school, based upon interviews in both generations. The correlation was statistically significant for the entire sample and for three status levels. This finding is consistent with the results obtained by Hodge and Treiman for intergenerational transmission of joining characteristics from parents to their adult children. Robert W. Hodge and Donald J. Treiman, "Social Participation and Social Status," *American Sociological Review* 33: 733. Hodge and Treiman, however, apparently used adults' recall of their parents' participation, which seems to be a dubious procedure.

16. This kind of yearly termination and cashing in is similar to the organizational mode noted in the mutual-aid lodge.

17. Unless one would include Frazier's excellent *Black Bourgeoisie,* with its commentary on the social life of the Negro white-collar class.

18. Community newspapers, as contrasted to metropolitan papers, stress local news and define their function in relation to what metropolitan papers do not cover. Social events therefore are of greater proportional significance in Negro and ethnic papers. One could easily overestimate from this the proportion of attention that Negro newspapers actually give to social events. At the same time, the extensive coverage given to these events may have the consequence for Negroes of distorting their self-image as a people. There is a recurrent rumor in the research city that the management of the Negro paper and the metropolitan papers have made a deal not to invade each other's territory in news coverage. Whether or not this is true, the metropolitan papers do not cover Negro social events and the press remains one of the most segregated of all American institutions. On Negro newspapers, the best sources are: Myrdal, *American Dilemma;* Frazier, *Black Bourgeoisie.*

19. See Charles Keil, *Urban Blues;* Elliott Liebow, *Tally's Corner: A Study of Negro Streetcorner Men.*

20. The history of the NAACP has been presented in many documents. The best brief account is by Langston Hughes, *Fight For Freedom: The Story of the NAACP.*

21. Whitney Young, *To Be Equal.*

22. E. U. Essien-Udom, *Black Nationalism;* Eric Lincoln, *The Black Muslims in America;* Louis E. Lomax, *When the Word is Given.*

23. Little has been written on the SCLC itself, although much appears in writings by and about King. See Martin Luther King, Jr., *Stride Toward Freedom; Strength To Love; Why We Can't Wait; Where Do We Go From Here?*

24. Inge Powell Bell, *CORE and the Strategy of Non-Violence.*

25. Howard Zinn, *SNCC: The New Abolitionists;* Jack Newfield, *A Prophetic Minority.*

26. Mizruchi examined such phenomena in his study of anomie and organizational life (Ephraim Mizruchi, *Success and Opportunity*, p. 112).

27. The concept of the "upward skidder" is found in W. B. Cameron, *Informal Sociology*, pp. 93–106.

28. Attendance intensivity could be conceptualized and measured. However, it proves to be difficult to use in practice, since the number of combinations of belonging to types and relative frequency of attendance in them is great.

4

WHAT
NEGROES
BELONG TO

In this chapter we return to the method of analysis established in chapter 2. In that chapter we were concerned with the relationship of a group of variables that we designated as social relationships (coracialism, reinforcement, and collegiality) and the frequency of membership in voluntary associations analyzed by social status. The problem now becomes more complex as we search for associations of these same variables and the amount of membership in each specific kind of voluntary association.

We found in chapter 2 that occupational status was a

consistent general predictor of amount of membership. The major difference in amount of membership was that between the white-collar and the blue-collar sets. We also found that coracialism was positively related to amount of membership for the whole sample but collegiality and reinforcement were not. When we examined the social relations concepts at each occupational status level we found that coracialism remained important and that among white-collar workers, collegiality was associated with membership.

In an attempt to explain the remaining variance, we turned to respondents' "type of employment" (an operational form of "authority," treated in chapter 1). Among the more important findings were that the white-collar company-employed belonged more often than the self-employed, and the low blue-collar person-employed belonged more often than company-employed. In addition to the use of type of employer, we used certain attributes as controls, such as sex and status as head of household and found further interesting variations due to social relationship variables. We concluded that the general theory about the correlation of social relationships and membership advanced in chapter 1 was adequate when the conditions under which the relationships occurred were adequately specified. We therefore decided to carry out the remainder of the analysis with the social relationship variables of coracialism, reinforcement, and collegiality as basic elements.

Accordingly, in chapter 3, additional dimensions of the dependent variable (amount of membership) were conceived, such as intensivity and extensivity. Variations in attendance and office-holding also were examined in detail, and their relations with intensivity and extensivity were tentatively explored.

In chapter 1 we put forward three general hypotheses derived from our theory. The first had to do with the causes of the amount of membership; the second with the type of voluntary association in which membership took place; the third with the ancillary effects of collegiality.

These are, of course, related, since by membership in kind of organization we refer to one of the ten types comprising the overall membership.

It is imperative that the issue of coracialism and membership be examined further, since the claim that coracialism is related to higher membership for the total sample, but that it is related to higher membership in only one kind of voluntary association, is apparently nonsensical. The problem lies in the nature of the organized approximations necessary in this kind of research. There are several possible explanations, each of which has significant consequences. First, it may be that the correlation of coracialism and Negro-rights membership is so strong that the association for the total membership of the sample is due to that component alone. In this case the expected finding would be a significant correlation of coracialism and Negro-rights membership and nonsignificant correlations for the other nine kinds. Our attention would then be directed to the reexamination of the procedures of chapter 2 to ascertain if parts of the irregular results found there were due to the nature of the organizations themselves rather than the social relationships.

Second, it may be that more than one kind of voluntary association membership is related to coracialism in any of several combinations—the problem then is to find adequate explanations for the correlations either in the independent variable and its correlates or in similarities in the types of organizations. In the latter case the distinction between expressive and instrumental voluntary associations would be indicated, since the character of instrumentality is basic to Negro-rights organizations.

The reasoning suggested here would apply to the findings for collegiality as well. The issue here is the unexpected finding that collegiality was related to membership among the white-collar set.

OCCUPATIONAL STATUS AND TYPE OF MEMBERSHIP

In order to visualize the kinds of problems to which this chapter is addressed, two arrangements of data are necessary. The first is from the perspective of the worker (Table 11), and shows the proportion of each occupational status set that belongs to each kind of organization. The second is from the perspective of the organization (Table 12) and shows what proportion of white-collar and blue-collar workers make up each type of organization.

Following Table 11, for each type of voluntary association (except sports) white-collar respondents have a higher membership than do blue-collar or the unemployed. Thus, the occupational status differences found for overall voluntary association membership are also found for memberships within nine of the ten types of voluntary associations.

Within each occupation category, the percentage of respondents belonging to each type of voluntary association is similar to that obtained when the occupational control was not employed (i.e., in comparison to the total). The major

TABLE 11

MEMBERSHIP BY OCCUPATIONAL STATUS IN TEN
TYPES OF VOLUNTARY ASSOCIATIONS (PERCENTS)

	White-collar	High blue-collar	Low blue-collar	Not working	Total
Church-related (E)[a]	33[c]	20	20	18	21
Regular lodge (E)	17	10	8	12	10
Mutual-aid lodge (I)[b]	15	10	6	6	8
Veterans' (E)	3	3	1	1	1
PTA (I)	22	10	9	12	12
Political (I)	2	1	<1	1	1
Professional, business and service (I)	25	2	1	2	4
Sports and athletic (E)	3	3	1	1	2
Social clubs (E)	9	4	3	4	4
Negro-rights (I)	37	5	8	2	11
Belong to at least one V.A.	77	44	38	37	44
N	(150)	(276)	(519)	(141)	(1,086)

[a] E = expressive.
[b] I = instrumental.
[c] The figures are the percentages in each cell of those who belong.

difference occurs in the Negro-rights category, where those who are not working have only one-quarter the membership of the low blue-collar. In general, the strong effect of class distinction can be seen throughout.

The two types of lodges reveal an interesting contrast in membership profiles. A decrease in membership is re-

TABLE 12

STATUS COMPOSITION OF TEN TYPES
OF VOLUNTARY ASSOCIATIONS (PERCENTS)

	White-collar	High blue-collar	Low blue-collar	Not working	Total
Church- **related (E)**[a]	21.1 (49)[c]	23.2 (54)	44.5 (103)	11.2 (26)	100.0 (232)
Regular **lodge (E)**	22.5 (26)	25.2 (28)	36.9 (43)	15.4 (17)	100.0 (114)
Mutual-aid **lodge (I)**[b]	25.2 (22)	31.1 (27)	34.5 (30)	9.2 (8)	100.0 (87)
Veterans' (E)	—[d]	—	—	—	(12)
PTA (I)	26.0 (33)	22.0 (28)	38.6 (49)	13.4 (17)	100.0 (127)
Political (I)	—	—	—	—	— (7)
Professional **business and** **service (I)**	75.5 (37)	10.2 (5)	8.2 (4)	6.1 (3)	100.0 (49)
Sports (E)	—	—	—	—	— (14)
Social clubs (E)	31.2 (14)	24.4 (11)	33.3 (15)	11.1 (5)	100.0 (45)
Negro-rights (I)	47.5 (55)	12.9 (15)	37.1 (43)	2.6 (3)	100.1 (116)
Percent of Total **Occupational** **Status**	13.8	25.4	47.8	13.0	100

[a] E = expressive.
[b] I = instrumental.
[c] The figures in parentheses are the number of cases represented by the percentages.
[d] Dash means less than 1 percent, when rounded.

lated to a decrease in occupational status, except that regular lodges show a "J" curve increase, due to a relatively high membership among those who are not working. A thorough exploration of each type would be required to find the reason for this, but the reputation of Negro regular lodges for helping the poor may be the explanation. Mutual-aid lodges, on the other hand, are a self-help group, and un-employment or irregular income would be likely to hinder joining. The greater proportion of lower status members in regular lodges very nearly accounts for the minor differences in total membership in the two kinds of lodges.

For most purposes, the blue-collar groups could be merged without much loss of information about who joins. When this is done, white-collar occupations have joining rates between one-and-a-half and two times that of the blue-collar and not-working. The major exceptions are the professional and business type which, as explained above, are mostly white-collar, and the Negro-rights type, which is much more sharply differentiated by occupation.

We now turn to an examination of our three hypotheses for the ten types of voluntary associations. As before, we will examine serially the relationships for coracialism, reinforcement, and collegiality. In this chapter such analysis will be facilitated if we do so within each status level.

WHITE-COLLAR

Among white-collar respondents, those with high coracialism more often joined church-related, PTA, professional, and

Negro-rights voluntary associations than those with low co-racialism.[1] For white-collar respondents, there was no relationship between coracialism and the other types of voluntary association membership. The significant result in the Negro-rights category verifies hypothesis 1 for this group, but the uneven finding for the others calls for explanation along the lines suggested at the start of the chapter.

Reference to Table 11 suggests examination of the fact that these four kinds of organizations have in common the highest membership rates, and it may be that the increment of joining them is due to the combined effects of coracialism and the other variables. Also, individuals who join any of these kinds of organizations may join them in these combinations. It should be recalled that this distinction between the person as actor and the memberships in the organizations in the community formed the analytical procedure in chapter 2. That is, coracialism may relate to the person, not to the membership.

The greater the intensivity, the less likely are multiple membership combinations, since there is a practical limit on the number of local organizations that a single person can join and participate in. Professional and business organizations are high in intensivity, but PTA and Negro-rights are low in intensivity. This lead is inconclusive.

Even though we cannot deal with the problem conclusively at this point, its significance should not be overlooked. If coracialism is causal only regarding memberships, the significance for the Negro community is quite different than if it is causal regarding increased diffuse participation of the person. The former would (among other things) point to specificity of norms regarding white-Negro relationships, in certain organizations, that pose a threat to white dominance. The latter interpretation would agree with the conclusion that Negroes with coracialism have greater freedom and latitude of action. Such an issue is not to be resolved simply by the obvious expedient of asking Negroes about threats on the job, even if such a recourse were feasible, since the effects of coracialism may be quite indirect or even not perceived.

The evidence regarding combinations of church-related, professional and business, Negro-rights, and PTA groups is that multiple memberships do not appear in these combinations in significant proportions. It seems likely that coracialism is related to each for separate reasons (to be explored below), and that when each is understood in detail, there is little reason to assume that coracialism is related in a general way to some personal tendency to diffuse pluralism. Rather, our thesis about coracialism is verified, but it must be seen in combination with other factors.

Reinforcement was not significantly related to total membership among white-collar respondents, which we assume is due to the generally weak position of unions among white-collar workers. We would not expect it to be related, therefore, to Negro-rights membership nor to the other three types correlated with coracialism. Teachers, numerically our largest professional group, belong much more often to the National Education Association, a voluntary association, than to the American Federation of Teachers or the United Federation of Teachers. For no type was there a significant association between reinforcement and membership.

In chapter 2 we found that collegiality was related to membership in voluntary associations only among white-

collar respondents. Before turning to the results for each type
of voluntary association, we again call attention to a problem associated with use of the concept of collegiality. Our
theoretical argument does not differentiate between those who
have low collegiality because of the isolation of their jobs
and those who have low collegiality for personality or social
reasons.

For white-collar respondents, those with high collegiality
more often joined Negro-rights, professional, business and
service, PTA, and church-related groups. These results cor-
respond to those for coracialism.

The effect of collegiality may differ for the professional
and the remainder of the white-collar. In chapter 2 we found
this to be true when total membership was considered. Here
it will be possible to sharpen the analysis by differentiating
among types of voluntary associations.

When collegiality for white-collar workers is analyzed
separately for professional and the remainder of the white-
collar (i.e., managers, proprietors, officials, and clerical and
sales), we find it associated only with the church-related type
of membership. Among white-collar nonprofessionals collegiality is now related only to membership in regular lodges.
When this same procedure is followed for coracialism, it is
found that among professionals high coracialism is related
to high rates of membership in PTA, professional, and business and service voluntary associations. There are no significant associations for the nonprofessional category. These results are summarized in Table 13.

In summary, there seem to be two kinds of effects among
Negro professionals: those with high coracialism join the
PTA, professional, and business and service voluntary asso-

TABLE 13

ASSOCIATION OF CORACIALISM, COLLEGIALITY,
AND MEMBERSHIP BY ORGANIZATIONAL TYPE, FOR
WHITE-COLLAR, PROFESSIONAL, NONPROFESSIONAL[a]

	CORACIALISM			COLLEGIALITY		
	White-collar	Profes-sional	Non-profes-sional	White-collar	Profes-sional	Non-profes-sional
Church-related	+[b]	0[c]	0	+	+	0
Regular lodges	0	0	0	0	0	+
PTA	+	+	0	+	0	0
Professional, business, and service	+	+	0	+	0	0
Negro-rights	+	0	0	+	0	0
All ten associations	+	0	0	+	+	0

[a] Omitted voluntary association types are zero in all columns. All significant associations were positive, i.e., those with high coracialism (or collegiality) had a higher percentage of membership in voluntary associations.
[b] + = statistically significant.
[c] 0 = not significant.

ciations, and those with high collegiality join church-related organizations. White-collar nonprofessionals have one salient characteristic in this regard: they join regular lodges when they have many friendship ties that connect work and community.

In chapter 2 we examined the nonprofessional white-collar workers and we found that there was no relationship between coracialism or collegiality and total voluntary association membership. The nonprofessional white-collar category includes clerical and sales as well as managers and proprietors, which may differ considerably in significant ways. Therefore, let us set aside the clerical and sales category and compare managers, proprietors, and officials with professionals. The findings are, first, that the professional in general joins more often but concentrates in particular types such as church-related, mutual-aid lodges, and Negro-rights types of organizations that professionals as well as managers, proprietors and officials join, but which professionals join about twice as often. Also, there are some voluntary associations that managers, proprietors, and officials rarely join but which professionals often join—the PTA and professional and business organizations. The data comparing professionals with managers, proprietors, and officials are presented in Table 14.

Coracialism is found to be diffusely related to white-collar participation in Negro-rights groups, and not to a particular white-collar occupation.[2] Since Negro teachers (and comparable professionals) are numerically a crucial group in the analysis of white-collar workers, it is germane to ask whether structural characteristics of their employment are responsible for the finding, rather than the qualities of their occupation. For example, since teachers work for large organizations they categorically have the opportunity for collegiality, and because most schools are segregated, Negro teachers often have high coracialism as well. If we classify white-collar workers according to the nature of the employer, we can determine whether the relationships found for coracialism and collegiality are true of the occupational status or are only a structural property of the type of organization within which the occupation is pursued. Accordingly we applied a distinction used in chapter 2 between

TABLE 14

MEMBERSHIP IN TEN TYPES OF VOLUNTARY
ASSOCIATIONS: PROFESSIONALS VS. MANAGERS,
PROPRIETORS, AND OFFICIALS

	ONE OR MORE ORGANIZATIONS OF TYPE, IN PERCENTS	
	Managers, Proprietors, and Officials	Professionals
Church-related	24	42
Regular lodge	20	19
Mutual-aid lodge	12	21
Veterans'	5	2
PTA	7	46
Political	2	3
Professional, business and service	3	58
Sports	—	7
Social clubs	10	12
Negro-rights	24	56
Total membership	55	88
N	(59)	(57)

self-employed, company-employed (any corporate employer, whether or not for profit), and person-employed (by an entrepreneur, in a household, client of a patron, and the like). A distinction was also made about number of employees of the employer, but this did not prove in practice to differ from the findings for type of employer.

There were too few person-employed white-collar workers for aggregate analysis. The data reveal that com-

pany-employed white-collar workers were more likely than
the self-employed to join church-related, PTA, and professional voluntary associations. There is no type to which the
self-employed belonged more frequently than did the company-employed. We might have expected that, for business
reasons, the self-employed would belong more frequently
than the company-employed to fraternal associations. Since
we also found that the nonprofessional white-collar more
frequently were members of regular lodges when they had
high collegiality, we may conclude that the small businessman with no colleagues at work has no structural social relations that channel him to organizational participation, so
far as work is concerned, though other causes may guide his
behavior. This finding is important: rational self-interest does
not prove to lead the businessman to participate; when he
has colleagues the ensuing social relations result in membership. We recognize that alternative explanations might be
offered, and this interpretation must be viewed as tentative,
but in general the results seem to support our thesis of the
significance of social relations at work for voluntary association membership.[3]

HIGH BLUE-COLLAR

When we examined the distribution of membership in types
of voluntary associations by occupational status, we found
that there was little distinction between blue-collar workers
and the not-working respondents as to proportion who
joined the various types. This does not justify the assump-

tion that coracialism, reinforcement, and collegiality have uniform effects among them. In fact, we have reason to assume that these occupational status categories differ considerably in structural qualities, with many of the high blue-collar working among whites or with white supervisors, many of the low blue-collar working in labor gangs of Negroes, a wide variation in size of employer, and so on. Consequently, we will examine the working-class occupational status sets separately and in detail, in roughly the same order as before.

Among high blue-collar respondents, none of the types of voluntary association memberships proves to be related to coracialism. This is not unexpected, since we previously found peculiarities in the relationship among high blue-collar workers between coracialism and total voluntary association membership. Part of the difficulty with the high blue-collar occupational category is that there are very few cases of high coracialism ($N = 21$). Since this might affect our results, we collapsed this high coracialism set with the medium. With this adjustment, a relationship now is found for the Negro-rights type of association, but the direction is reversed: those with high and medium coracialism combined join less often than do those with low coracialism. Examination of Table 5 (chapter 2) discloses the immediate reason for this. The bulk of the high blue-collar are in the medium coracialism category, and this category has the lowest percent of voluntary association members of the high blue-collar coracialism categories. Thus, had we combined the high and medium categories, there would have been only 42 percent memberships for this combined coracialism category compared to 46 percent for the low.

No statistically significant relationship was discovered for the other types of associations. Thus, high blue-collar respondents not only deviate from hypothesis 1 by demonstrating no positive relationship between coracialism and any type of voluntary association, but for Negro-rights voluntary associations, there is a relationship contrary to the hypothesis.

As noted previously, the high blue-collar is a composite category that combines skilled and semiskilled workers in order to have enough cases for analysis. Therefore, we examined separately the skilled and the remainder of the high blue-collar workers. That is, the relationship between coracialism and each type of voluntary association was examined within each of these occupational categories. However, this analysis does not alter the previous results: there is still no relationship between coracialism and any type of voluntary association within either the skilled or the semiskilled sets.

To emphasize the importance of this, we should restate these findings in more concrete terms. When Negro workers in jobs like truck driving, equipment operating, carpentry, masonry, electronics, machine repair, and so on have Negro supervisors or Negro coworkers, they less often join Negro-rights organizations than when they work only among whites. We should not misconstrue this as necessarily a case of defiance of whites, a mass movement of the isolated, or similar phenomena, because it is simultaneously true that the total membership of high blue-collar workers in Negro-rights groups is not large ($N = 15$ or 5.5 percent of the total) and is significantly less than membership among white-collar workers. As with white-collar workers, we shall pursue the course of examination of other work-related variables before attempting a more comprehensive explanation.

For high blue-collar respondents, reinforcement is directly associated with membership in Negro-rights voluntary associations. This precise reversal of the finding for coracialism, which tends to be generally similar in effect to reinforcement, is striking. Again referring to the components of the index, it seems likely that the issue centers around the role of the union: coracialism, which is a phenomenon of informal relations, is negatively related; reinforcement, a phenomenon of extrasystemic power, is effective. Because of the opposing independent effects of coracialism and reinforcement, we would expect some kind of cancellation effect for a combined coracialism and reinforcement index. This is the case. The data reveal no significant relationships between coracialism-reinforcement and membership in any kind of voluntary association.[4] We must conclude for high blue-collar workers that reinforcement does not augment coracialism relative to each type of organization. Our attention must now be directed to the unexpectedly strong role of union and civil service as an independent extrasystemic force contrasted with the weak or negative effect of coracialism, an informal relation.

We would expect collegiality, another measure of informal social relations, to be similar in effect to coracialism. The data reveal that high collegiality is not related to high rates of membership in any type of voluntary association, but that it closely approaches statistical significance for Negro-rights organizations. Collegiality is perhaps similar (we have no statistical confirmation) to union and civil service in its effect. Apparently the mere presence of others or their posi-

tion in the work hierarchy does not back up a worker in joining Negro-rights organizations, but affirmation of friendship
and outside power is decisive. It may be that among high blue-
collar Negro workers, Negro supervisors are Uncle Toms who
are obligated to whites for their jobs or positions, and the only
effective backing a worker has is external force and selective
friendship, which need not include supervisors.

In order to ascertain whether the conditions under
which skilled and semiskilled people work have different
effects, they were divided for separate analysis. The membership in Negro-rights organizations of the subsets were rather
small and of almost identical proportions. Apparently the
findings are not explainable in this fashion.

Almost all of the high blue-collar workers are company-
employed, and therefore we cannot examine comparatively
the effects of type of employer.

LOW BLUE-COLLAR

For low blue-collar respondents there is no relationship
between coracialism and any given type of voluntary association membership. Statistical significance is almost reached
for church-related, PTA, and Negro-rights associations, where
those with high coracialism join more often than do those
with low.

For low blue-collar workers, the relationship (described
in chapter 2) between coracialism and voluntary association
membership apparently is not strong enough to be maintained for any of the separate types of voluntary associations.
This is not surprising, since we have already shown (see

Table 12) that there is only one voluntary association type that enrolls a substantial number of low blue-collar members. For low blue-collar respondents hypothesis 1 is not supported, although for Negro-rights organizations the relationship approaches statistical significance. Following the reasoning for high blue-collar workers, we might expect this to be due to the importance of reinforcement. This does not prove to be the case. Reinforcement is not related to membership in any type of voluntary association, although the result again comes close to statistical significance for Negro-rights associations.

For the combined occupational status categories, we found no relationship between collegiality and membership frequency. For low blue-collar workers, there is no reason to assume differentials in this regard among voluntary association types. For church-related organizations, low blue-collar workers with high collegiality less often belong than do those with low collegiality (we do not consider those who work alone). Although this result was unexpected, it does not seem out of the ordinary when we consider the constituency of the low blue-collar category. There is a large component of female workers among the set, and they are heavily involved in domestic day-labor and short-term employment in which social relationships are transitory. At the same time, they are more often church members than are comparable men (for reasons perhaps unrelated to work) and are more often involved in church-related voluntary associations mediated through community rather than through work-social relations. In order to examine this further, let us turn to the data regarding type of employer of low blue-collar workers.

Person-employed low blue-collar workers more often

belong to church-related voluntary associations than do company-employed. Since many person-employed respondents are women, removing women from the sample should alter the results. This proves to be the case: among low blue-collar males who are heads of households, there is no relationship between type of employment and membership in church-related voluntary associations. However, 305 of the 327 males in the category are company-employed, and we must keep in mind the joint effects previously found of being male and company-employed.

Females who work alone at domestic employment for whites are not only isolated from other workers but are in a vulnerable position regarding expression of their views. This is not necessarily the case for males in company situations, although it may frequently be the case. Hence it is surprising to find that person-employed low blue-collar males belong to Negro-rights organizations more often than company-employed males. However, for low blue-collar company-employed males there is no relationship between coracialism and overall membership in voluntary associations, while for low blue-collar person-employed males there is a positive relationship between coracialism and overall membership. What this means is that person-employed males having Negro supervisors and Negro coworkers are more likely to belong to voluntary associations. The apparent anomaly of person-employed blue-collar males more frequently joining Negro-rights associations has a simple explanation in terms of coracialism, as hypothesis 1 would lead us to expect.[5]

THOSE WHO DO NOT WORK

There were 141 respondents (13 percent of the total) who were reported as "not working." It should be recalled that the sampling method was designed not to discover how many residents were unemployed, but to select for analysis household heads who were twenty to sixty years of age. Only in residences with no family members twenty to sixty who worked was a person interviewed who was not working. Thus we have not included people who were not working if some other appropriate person in that household did work. Consequently, our sample probably overselects not-working people in those households where lack of work is a serious problem. We did not rigorously distinguish between members of the labor force who were not working temporarily and the general reserve of adults who will work when work appears to offer a clear advantage, but ordinarily do not work. For our research, the problem was the consequence of the absence of social relations, and although the not-working otherwise lack homogeneity, they do have this major factor in common. At any rate, the category is numerically large and contains almost as many respondents as the entire white-collar set.[6]

It was mentioned previously that the not-working were mostly low blue-collar when they did work. Their distribution of memberships does not vary markedly from the low blue-collar set. Coracialism and collegiality are, by definition, impossible for the not-working, although some respondents did answer according to the conditions they experienced when they last worked. However, there did not prove to be any relationships between either coracialism or collegiality and voluntary association membership.

Reinforcement is logically possible for those who were not working. A large number of low blue-collar males in the research city are longshoremen and all are union members. They frequently have periods of unemployment. Where the respondent had been working recently as a longshoreman and expected to work again he was counted as employed.

Thus one major source of union, and hence reinforcement classification, was not found among the not-working, and they have fewer other sources of reinforcement as well. There were no cases where reinforcement was associated with high rates of joining a type of voluntary association.

The similarity of voluntary association memberships of low blue-collar and not-working sets perhaps testifies to the precarious state of the former. A large number of low blue-collar workers are temporary or casual employees and simply happened to consider themselves as working the day the interviewer knocked at the door. It was merely a matter of chance that they fell into one set rather than the other.

What, for instance, would be the meaning of coracialism for a Negro male manual laborer in Tampa who gets his work by standing on Nebraska Avenue and waiting for a man in a truck to stop and shout "Anyou boys wanta work?" He knows as much about the employer as the authors or the reader. The work may turn out to be any kind of physical labor, such as unloading a truck. His payment is in cash, at a rate unknown to him. Although such employers may be legally obliged to deduct and file social security taxes, often they do not do so. Collegiality in such circumstances can have little force. A similar situation prevails for city-resident laborers who do occasional work in citrus processing or picking, although in these cases it is more likely that minimum wage laws will be observed. If the employer does not have any fear of sanction, neither does he offer security.

In short, there seems to be a need for examination of the nature of the quality of coracialism as well as its presence. Collegiality was intended to be this kind of variable —a measure of quality or strength of relations, just as coracialism was a measure of solidarity in a society characterized by segregation. It is apparent, however, that friends can be powerless, and racial unity can be a negative factor under conditions too often encountered by blue-collar workers.

Does the long-term unemployed person have any unique social relations that strengthen his connection with the community and with specific voluntary associations? The list to be examined would include those helping agencies that become the substitute source of funds. The welfare recipient leaves the emploity when he goes "on the welfare" and enters a world of required relationships with welfare agents. If welfare agencies were actually social-work agencies, there might be a basis for examining them as cryptoreinforcement sources. They are not. For the most part, welfare agencies are seen by welfare recipients as foes to be deceived regarding a multitude of frustrating rules. To be a long-term unemployed man or woman is to became part of the inverse elite, and like any elite, to be held up for examination of quality: to have one's name in the antisocial register (the AFDC central file), to have one's lineage checked for legitimacy just like the upper-elite, to go to select schools, to develop a unique language and subculture, to have a highly limited group of friends—but not to join organizations that operate outside these kinds of limits.

In some such cases, a long-term socialization to inverse-elite standing takes place, with the welfare agencies becoming parent substitutes for adults who are in permanent dependency. Such persons do not look to community organizations as instrumentalities for change, but look to their parent substitutes for favors. Their ambition is not a better job, but a successful con. One such person came to one of the writers (as a social worker in another city) with a problem about the neighbors. His face was livid as he paced the floor. His indignation grew as he thought aloud. His language of threats was not what *he* would do, however, but this: "Why, I've got the welfare behind me, the Veterans Administration behind me, the Legion behind me, the Salvation Army behind me, the. . . ." He pounded the desk as he expounded his list of substitute big brothers that are bigger than your big brothers.

This type of welfare dependent does not channel his need through voluntary associations as a member, though as we have seen there is a slight tendency for increased membership in regular lodges that have a charity function. The relationship of voluntary associations with such people is more often through staff contact or a service committee of volunteers, but not typically through membership. In chapter 3 we stressed the equal status aspect of voluntary association members, and by this definition the charity recipient cannot be viewed as a member.[7]

CONCLUSIONS

The consistent confirmation of hypotheses among white-collar workers about the importance of social relationships conceptualized as coracialism, reinforcement, and collegiality must be seen in combinations with their patterns of intensivity, attendance, and officership discovered in chapter 3. A picture then emerges of pluralistic white-collar Negroes, who work in large organizations and who are strongly oriented toward leadership in instrumental or social influence organizations, (notably Negro-rights groups), when they have coracialism, collegiality, and outside backing. Whether or not their leadership is effective is another issue, but the fact that their work is among other Negroes and their participation is in Negro organizations indicates that black pluralism has many natural barriers to overcome before it can make a significant contribution to white society, as well as black.

Second, the statistically significant relations between social relationships and membership among white-collar workers is strongly influenced by the availability of voluntary associations that are both large and heavily middle class, namely the professional and Negro-rights types. In contrast, the organizations to which blue-collar workers belong tend to be class-diffuse, with many blue-collar workers as members but often led by white-collar participants. White-collar workers with coracialism join Negro-rights organizations as a direct outcome of the presence of many other Negroes at work and the collegiality made possible by the permanence and stability of that work; when they join voluntary associations that are class-diffuse, they often are leaders there.

The particularistic and detailed nature of the operation of coracialism and reinforcement among blue-collar workers, compared to the consistent nature of these variables among the white-collar set, is perhaps just another example of the greater difficulties faced by lower-class workers in general. The number of situations favorable to their frequent participation are few and scattered, and the barriers to participation are many.

Negro-rights organizations, along with the professional, and business and service voluntary associations, emerge as those most specifically related to the social-relations variables, largely because of the inconsistent joint effects among the white-collar workers and the white-collar nature of the voluntary associations themselves. Of these two organization types, the professional, and business and service are bound up with the control of the voluntary associations by whites. Only the Negro-rights organizations have unimpeded direct relevance to the total Negro community because they alone are both by and for Negroes. In the next chapter we turn to a more comprehensive examination of the feelings of the entire Negro community about these Negro-rights organizations and membership in them.

NOTES

1. A graph of the relationship between coracialism and church-related voluntary association membership would be somewhat U-shaped. However, the principal variation in such mem-

bership was between those with "medium" coracialism (who belong more often than under the null expectation), and those with "low" (who belong less often than expected).

2. A methodological comment is in order, which has relevance throughout our work but is illustrated pointedly here. The phenomenon of a significant relation between values of two variables A and B and a nonsignificant relationship between two subpopulations A' and A" and B is not unusual and not technically incorrect. It indicates that separate properties of subsamples A' and A" have been grouped by rearrangement of the cases into a different order by following some introduced criteria. In chapter 2 we found a similar phenomenon, only in reverse sequence: we constructed two sets of voluntary associations (instrumental and expressive) from an original set of ten, and by so doing we discovered independent properties of instrumental organizations as a whole. This kind of latent structure analysis is made more problematic by the merely conventional reasons for assuming that only an arbitrary, fixed level of probability is significant.

3. This section also bears on the issue of whether cause of joining is integrated in the person or is concrete and particularistic. As before, the weight of evidence supports the latter conclusion.

4. It should be noted that for many of these types of organizations the direction of the relationship is as predicted but the number of cases is too small to say, on a probability basis, that there is a relationship (technically, that we are sampling from a population in which there is a relationship).

5. In the section on white-collar workers and in note 3 we asked if evidence would confirm the idea that the causes of membership affected the person as a whole, or affected only the membership of the person. The argument can now be rejoined with evidence from blue-collar workers. The finding seems to be that the issue concerns white-collar workers alone because so few blue-collar workers belong to more than one organization.

6. It is tempting to assume that when the unemployed become more numerous than the white-collar workers, a crucial

point in the viability of a community has been reached. Perhaps there is some truth in this kind of observation, but to evaluate it is another matter. Demographers have found it useful to calculate a ratio between the number of economically productive people and the number of nonproductive people in a society as an index of the economic problems that the unit faces. In a similar way we might calculate a ratio of the number of voluntary associations at one stratum to the number at another stratum, but again, we do not have the basic criteria from which to make a judgment about its meaning.

7. At this point in the book, we planned a section on the association of social relationships and instrumental or expressive memberships. The reasons for its absence are instructive. First, only among white-collar workers are there enough cases for analysis of multiple membership, but the white-collar workers who belong to two or more groups frequently belong to both types. Second, the concepts of instrumental and expressive are not useful when single organizations or types dominate communities—such is the case with the class-diffuse church-related (expressive) or class-biased Negro-rights (instrumental). Third, we have shown the specificity of causation of membership, and it would be fallacious to group these concrete connections between work and joining of constructed categories; even if a pattern emerged, it would not necessarily be true for other communities with different organizational patterns.

5

NEGRO-RIGHTS
VOLUNTARY
ASSOCIATIONS

The institutions of a community are interrelated. In the
preceding chapters we have delineated many of the important social aspects of the Negro communities of Tampa,
and we have seen emerging a picture of both the sociological
generality and the uniqueness in human terms of the institutional sets of race, emploity, church, and voluntary associations.

In this intricate network, the community-related uniqueness of each kind of voluntary association comes into focus
in the way that lodges adjust to the need for security in a

segregated society; the way that church-related groups perform integrative functions; the ironic aspect of social clubs
in the absence of secure bases for power; the unique tie
between bureaucratic teachers, professional organizations, and
Parent-Teacher Associations, the special place of importance reserved for racially oriented voluntary associations,
and so on. Three kinds of voluntary associations must be
judged to be of prepotent significance in the Negro community: the church-related, as the secular arm of the all-
important church; the professional-PTA cluster, because of
the prominence of teachers and their intensive ties with white
and nonwhite organizations; and the Negro-rights, because
of their high prestige, widespread acceptance, and position as
spokesmen for Negroes to the more powerful white world.

We have selected Negro-rights organizations for special
attention because they, more than the others, represent the
uniqueness of the Negro community, qua Negro, because
they present its paradoxes and problems in accessible form,
and because (unlike churches and schools) all members of
the community have these few specific organizations in
common as the agents of their principal identity. Accordingly
we chose to ask more questions about Negro-rights organizations than about any others. These questions focused on attitudes about such organizations as well as membership in
them.

Read in conjunction with descriptions of the organizations themselves in chapter 3, this chapter constitutes a comprehensive multilevel case study of a single kind of Negro
organization. The analysis in this chapter is a miniature of
the entire book, applied to one kind of voluntary association.

PATTERNS OF MEMBERSHIP

Negro-Rights Organizations Among Others

To set the scene, let us briefly review and synthesize the available information about the place of Negro-rights organizations and membership.

Eleven percent of the respondents claimed membership in one or more Negro-rights organizations, which is identical to the proportion for regular lodges. Only two have greater proportions, the PTA with 12 percent and the church-related with 21 percent.

Negro-rights voluntary associations, on the other hand, have the lowest proportion of any type of organization of belongers who attend once a year—69 percent.[1] They have the lowest proportion of office-holders, a mere 3 percent. Negro-rights organizations rank somewhat higher in combined membership, attendance, and office-holding, ranking fourth in percentage of those who belong to two or more organizations and who also attend and hold office in at least one.

Negro-rights organizations rank second in the proportion of white-collar members, first place going to the professional and business and service. When we consider the specific normative linkages of the professional and business and service, and the restricted access to them on grounds of occupation and education, Negro-rights groups emerge as the single kind of open-access organization that enrolls a disproportionate number of high-status members. We found no voluntary association type that was, by contrast, weighted to low-status membership.

Negro-rights organizations have one added occupation-related feature, shared by no other type. They have a U-shaped membership curve, with a comparatively low number of middle-status members and much higher proportions of lower- and higher-status members. Social clubs have a slight tendency of this kind. These facts may be observed in Table 12.

The status specificity of Negro-rights voluntary associations can also be seen from the perspective of the occupational status set itself. Negro-rights is the kind of voluntary association membership most often claimed by white-collar workers and is the highest in this regard of any voluntary association type for any status level. Second in this regard is the church-related set, which, like professional organizations, has a normative link to another set of nonvoluntary associations, the churches.

Membership and Linkage

When the importance of normative links to formal organizations (associations, not voluntary associations) for success of voluntary associations is highlighted, one reason for the prominence of Negro-rights organizations becomes more apparent. They are tied with regular lodges for first place in membership of those voluntary associations that are not allied to another local structure (see Table 15).

The effect of linkage may be disputed, of course. Lodges and veterans have national ties, and some political clubs have direct political support. A few local social groups, such as fraternities, are nationally organized. Nevertheless, it is the

TABLE 15

MEMBERSHIP AND ATTENDANCE OF LINKED AND
NOT LINKED VOLUNTARY ASSOCIATIONS

	Respondents who belong %	Belongers who attend meetings[a] %
Linked		
Church-related	21	97
PTA	12	82
Professional, business, and service	5	90
Not Linked		
Regular lodges	11	91
Negro-rights	11	64
Mutual-aid lodges	8	86
Social clubs	4	98
Sports	2	95
Veterans'	2	75
Political	1	100

[a] Members who attend at least once a year.

sponsorship or captivity by a local structure that furnishes the strongest link, and the links with those organizations having economic power and public sanction or mandate are the most useful.[2]

The lack of such ties is one of the most significant features of Negro-rights organizations. Because of it, they must develop organizational features that supply the missing elements of power and sanction or mandate. Both the NAACP and the Urban League have courted the favor of prominent Negroes and whites, locally and nationally, and fund-raising is one of their perennial problems. Urban League branches frequently seek funds from welfare councils, community funds, and the like. When successful, the Urban League falls into the "linked" category, as is the case in Tampa. Of greatest importance for our research, both the NAACP and the Urban League are forced to become very conscious of the prestige-conferring capability of their organization and of its members. To do otherwise would be to lose a major source of support.

By contrast, teachers achieve their prominence not only because of their vital educational contribution, but also because they are salaried and their voluntary associations are approved by the schools they serve. Business voluntary associations may have the support of the Negro businessmen themselves, few though they be, but the organizations lack the uniformity of linkage and specific and defined common interest. Voluntary associations linked to big corporations are usually far better supported and are related to a role definition of the worker that allows greater participation. When, if ever, large corporations in the Negro community have black control, black capital, and black executives with community contact, then the NAACP and the Urban League will prosper (by which time they may not be needed).

NAACP MEMBERSHIP AND
SOCIAL RELATIONSHIPS AT WORK

Our theory about the causes of membership has been tested for the sample as a whole and for each of ten types of voluntary associations (not all reported directly), including

Negro-rights organizations as a set. We have seen that the NAACP and the Urban League are the vital core of Negro-rights voluntary associations in Tampa. If our theory is adequate, it should be able to explain membership in each of these organizations as well as in the category as a whole.

Only the NAACP is sufficiently large to provide a fully detailed analysis, so we will concentrate on it here. Later in the chapter we will compare more completely community opinion about the two. There is some reason to expect differences between them, although their membership proportions are similar. The NAACP has perhaps more often been involved in controversy and in direct conflict with whites, while the Urban League has stressed self-improvement, job training, and social adjustment. It would be easy to overstate these distinctions, however, and in recent years there has been a growing similarity in their militance, if not their programs. Of the two, the NAACP has had to be more concerned with membership, and its annual elections are usually intensely fought out in the organization and to some extent in the community. The Urban League, in contrast, has had a greater stability and continuity with less emphasis on membership, probably because it is partially financed by the United Fund. This has allowed the existence of an Urban League staff and headquarters and has made membership support less imperative. It is likely, therefore, that when we measure support by membership that we underestimate the strength of the Urban League compared with the NAACP.

NAACP and Membership

When considering social relationships by occupational status, we found that the correlations of the three variables with membership were most clear-cut for white-collar workers. Almost 40 percent of white-collar respondents said they belonged to the NAACP, while only 6.5 percent of the high blue-collar, 7.3 percent of the low blue-collar, and 2.1 percent of the not-working claimed membership. The status skewness of the entire Negro-rights category is heavily influenced by the NAACP component. We might expect, therefore, even stronger relationships between social-relationship variables and NAACP membership than for the entire Negro-rights set.

In order to facilitate later comparisons, only the data for males will be analyzed. The results in general are similar to those obtained for overall membership in voluntary associations. In the case of both white-collar and low-blue collar occupational sets, those with high coracialism more often belong to the NAACP than do those with low. The familiar U-shaped distribution appears among high blue-collar respondents; those with medium coracialism join the NAACP less frequently than do those with either high or low.

Patterns for collegiality are similar to those found for coracialism. Respondents with high collegiality more frequently join the NAACP among both the white-collar and low blue-collar occupational sets, but the direction of this relationship is reversed among high blue-collar respondents. High blue-collar respondents with the lowest collegiality (those who are isolated because they work alone) more often belong to the NAACP.

The correlation of reinforcement and NAACP membership is significant for low blue-collar and high blue-collar but not for white-collar respondents.

TABLE 16

HIGH BLUE-COLLAR MALES: CORACIALISM,
REINFORCEMENT, COLLEGIALITY,
AND NAACP MEMBERSHIP (PERCENTS)

	Coracialism	Collegiality	Reinforcement
High	11	6	13
	(18)[a]	(169)	(52)
Medium	4	8	(no
	(150)	(62)	category)
Low	12	16	6
	(83)	(19)	(196)
N[b]	(251)	(250)	(248)

[a] Figures in parentheses refer to the number of cases in the base.
[b] N varies due to variation in nonresponses.

In order to visualize what needs to be explained, let
us list the factors associated with joining NAACP.

  white-collar: high coracialism
                high collegiality
  high blue-collar: high coracialism
                low coracialism
                low collegiality (work alone)
                high reinforcement
  low blue-collar: high coracialism
                high collegiality
                high reinforcement

The only relationships contrary to our theory appear,
as before, among the high blue-collar, when the positive
effect on joining of low coracialism and low collegiality (or

isolation) require explanation. Only 6.5 percent of the 251
high blue-collar males belong, the lowest of any occupational
set, and none of the 18 high blue-collar women belong.
The workers are distributed unevenly, with 150 in the medium coracialism set (i.e., Negro coworkers but no Negro
supervisor). Only two high coracialism, high blue-collar
workers belong to the NAACP. The very uneven nature of
the high blue-collar category can be seen from inspection of
Table 16. A major factor in the unusual results is the ex-
tremely unbalanced composition of the low row; as in
chapter 4, the analysis seems to point to a latent structure
of subpopulations that cannot be identified with such a
small number of cases.[3]

NEGRO-RIGHTS ORGANIZATIONS: MEMBERSHIP AND ATTITUDES

What Attitudes Are

Since the meaning and use of such terms as attitude and
opinion have been quite varied, it is appropriate to state explicitly the usage to be employed in this book. Although it is
possible to develop a theoretical formulation for use here,
we will not do so. The limitations of field-research tech-
niques make such work largely fatuous because the theoretical implications could not be tested. To illustrate briefly, the
implications of a definition such as "an attitude is a predisposition to act in relation to a definition of the situation"
would involve operationalization of predisposition and defini-

tion of the situation, and some estimate of the meaning of predisposition in the cognitive and emotional structure of the person. Our aim is more modest. We want to know what Negroes say about their voluntary associations. In our research, we paid attention to just that: we asked questions about specific organizations and recorded the answers. Attitudes, for us, are simply the record of a verbal statement in the interview situation.[4]

Let us therefore expand upon our earlier brief mention of the nature of the interview situation. All interviews were conducted in the respondents' homes. Interviewers were Negroes with identical training. The interviewer was instructed to go to a predesignated dwelling and to interview there only the specified person. Up to eight callbacks were required before the attempt to conduct the interview could be abandoned. The time of the interview was dependent on the availability of the respondent and typically occurred in the afternoon or evening. No attempt was made to attain sexual homogeneity in the interview, except where female interviewers (rarely) invoked their option to have a male substitute. Since research on Negro communities has been frequently accused of undersampling Negro males, those details became matters of considerable importance: the rigorous application of the sampling design, the search of fringe areas, and the options available to female interviewers make it possible to state with confidence that adult males (not in institutional populations) were properly represented.

Operationally, then, an attitude is a recorded verbal statement made by a Negro respondent to a Negro interviewer, when contacted at home, under the conditions described above.[5]

Attitudes as Research Variables

"Evidence from many sources points to the very loose relationship between opinions or attitudes (as expressed in interviews and questionnaires) and subsequent behavior with regard to the objects of these opinions or attitudes."[6] We wholeheartedly agree with this statement by Williams. We will find, for example, that most Negroes in Tampa approve of the NAACP, but only about one-tenth join. It is obvious that the abstract statements made in an interview must be examined in relation to personality and mediating social structures before they can be utilized in prediction.

The stance of this chapter is that attitudes help expand our explanation of other variables. They are an added tool for understanding the meaning of the other things a person tells us. We do not have research methods that allow full examination of either the sources or the consequences of attitudes; rather we will examine attitudes themselves as a part of the explanation we offer about work and voluntary association membership. Hence we proceed by a virtual recapitulation of the topics we have already examined: the patterns of attitudes about belonging; the variations of attitudes with status; coracialism, reinforcement, and collegiality.

Membership and Attitudes

The theoretical issues regarding the relationship of attitudes and membership outlined above have practical counterparts. We assume that a statement that one belongs implies approval of joining (which may not be true outside the interview situation) and therefore those organizations that have high membership rates presumably have an initial large component of approval. We present the data in combined form, in Table 17, arranged in descending order according to the combined membership and approval rates.

TABLE 17

MEMBERSHIP IN AND APPROVAL OF
FIVE NEGRO-RIGHTS ORGANIZATIONS

	N	Would join or belongs %	Undecided %	Would not join %
NAACP	(1,084)	75.5	18.1	6.0
Urban League	(1,080)	53.5	34.7	12.0
CORE[a]	(1,077)	22.7	51.0	26.3
SNCC[a]	(1,077)	11.5	46.5	42.0
Black Muslims[a]	(1,081)	3.8	20.5	75.7

[a] Means negligible local membership.

These organizations are a mixed set, with NAACP and Urban League representing local membership organizations, CORE and SNCC mostly known only nationally, and the Black Muslims having a local membership that is negligible in the sample but well-known in the community. The symmetry of the table is notable: the lower the "would join or belongs" figure, the higher the "would not join," while the "undecided" column has approximately a normal statistical distribution. CORE and SNCC, which are not local, bring a high "undecided" response, while small "undecided" responses are found for those organizations that are either strongly approved or strongly disapproved.

If the proportion of actual membership in the NAACP

is subtracted from the "would join or belongs" column, the "would join" figures still show that the NAACP is more often favored than any other Negro-rights organization. For those with no local membership, the general tendency is for greater conventionality to be associated with greater approval.[7]

The large proportion of undecided responses may indicate lack of salience of at least the center three organizations in the table. If this is true for these three, and perhaps in lesser degree for the others, we must retain some reserve about the significance of an approval or disapproval, as well. To gain perspective on the characteristics of those who have an opinion, let us first dispose of the case of the people who do not. The undecided responses are displayed in Table 18. The organizations are placed in the same order as in Table

TABLE 18

UNDECIDED RESPONSES ABOUT FIVE NEGRO-RIGHTS ORGANIZATIONS BY OCCUPATIONAL STATUS[a]

	NAACP %	Urban League %	CORE %	SNCC %	Muslims %	Total %	N
White-collar	9.6	20.5	39.0	35.5	11.6	2.7	149
High blue-collar	17.9	32.1	51.0	43.9	18.3	6.5	277
Low blue-collar	18.6	39.2	52.9	51.9	21.6	6.8	515
All occupations	18.1	34.7	51.0	46.5	20.0		

[a] Cell totals by row vary slightly from previous figures due to nonresponses.

17. In Table 17 the phenomenon of equivalent proportions of indecision about strongly approved and strongly disapproved organizations was observed. In Table 18 we see a similar pattern by occupational status: the higher the occupational status, the less the indecision, although the blue-collar occupations are almost identical.

Indecision and the Mass Man

Our provisional theory, in chapter 1, was formed around Kornhauser's theme of mass society. For Kornhauser, the mass man is one who lacks involvement with "proximate concerns." By this Kornhauser means structured social relationships which mediate man and society, such as local government, clubs, and the like. In chapter 2 we contrasted the mass man and the pluralist man, as we encountered them in our research. The striking findings about indecision regarding Negro-rights organizations during an era of intense controversy over racial justice would seem to be an example of the thinking of the mass man in his apathy phase.

If the thinking we found can be attributed to the mass man, we would expect to find that those in our sample with no voluntary association memberships have the highest number of undecided responses regarding controversial Negro-rights groups, and that those with memberships would have opinions, favorable or unfavorable. Following the criteria in chapter 2, the respondents were divided into two sets: those with no memberships and those with two or more. It was found that indecision and not belonging were not related. Or, stated positively, those who belonged to two or more organizations were undecided about as often as those who did not belong at all. This was true for each of the five organizations, for white-collar, high blue-collar, low blue-collar, and not-working. It should be noted that the NAACP and the Urban League were counted among the two or more organizations a person could join. Yet, even though these are included among the memberships of pluralists, the relation of joining and indecision is not changed.

The observation that membership and indecision are unrelated can be checked independently by testing for a relationship between coracialism and indecision, since coracialism proved to be the best predictor of membership. Coracialism was not related to indecision.

SOCIAL RELATIONSHIPS AT WORK
AND ATTITUDES TO MEMBERSHIP

The findings about patterns of membership and patterns of indecision indicate that structural features of work that are most consistently related to joining are not related to opinion. Membership is a product of strong forces in the work situation, particularly those linkages that express the central purposes of the employee, the employer, and his enterprise, but attitudes appear to be the product of some other forces that we have not delineated.

Before we can have confidence in these conclusions, a more comprehensive examination of social relationships and the conditions under which they occur is necessary. Detailed data were obtained regarding the NAACP and the Urban League, the two organizations that had substantial membership and were well known in the community.

NAACP

Information about membership in a Negro-rights organization is mixed in the same index as information about approval of membership, because we assumed that joining signifies approval. Therefore, the results as to attitudes about joining are influenced by the differences in membership among the various occupational categories and within the categories of our independent variables (coracialism, reinforcement, and collegiality).

Among the white-collar and low blue-collar respondents, those with high coracialism more often say that they "would join or belong" to the NAACP. Coracialism is not related even to a willingness to belong to the NAACP among high blue-collar respondents.

In order to gain some precision in our findings, the reinforcement and collegiality variables were examined for males only. However, even with this control, union and/or civil-service status was not related to willingness to belong to the NAACP. Both white-collar and low blue-collar males belong or claim a greater willingness to join the NAACP if they have high collegiality.

Urban League

The Urban League, like the NAACP, may be considered to be a middle-class voluntary association but is less controversial than the NAACP among those whites who are familiar with it. Furthermore, the Urban League does not have a reputation for militancy, as does the NAACP, and despite its long history, it is among the less widely publicized Negro-rights organizations, at least among whites.

We noted earlier in the chapter that the Urban League is the second most widely approved Negro-rights association among our respondents. As with the NAACP, the relationship of coracialism to belonging plus willingness to join varies by occupational status. Those respondents with high coracialism would join or do belong to the Urban League regardless of their occupational status. High blue-collar respondents with low coracialism are more likely than those with other levels of coracialism to be willing to join. Those with medium coracialism are more likely than those with high or low coracialism to be undecided or to say they would not join. Among the low blue-collar, those with low coracialism more often say that they would not join.[8] Except for high blue-collar respondents, then, the higher the coracialism the more favorable are joining and opinions about joining the Urban League.

Reinforcement is not related to joining and willingness to join the Urban League within any occupational category. Since coracialism is related, we may assume that the significant joint effect of reinforcement and coracialism among the white-collar is due to the effect of coracialism alone.

Collegiality is positively related to joining and willingness to join the Urban League among both white-collar and low blue-collar respondents. It may be recalled that it was precisely among this group that collegiality was most strongly related to joining. These two variables are not so related among high blue-collar respondents.

Existing membership in other voluntary associations is positively related to willingness to join the Urban League among white-collar and low blue-collar respondents, but is not related among high blue-collar respondents. This suggests that the finding of a relationship between existing voluntary association memberships in general and willingness to join the NAACP is not due simply to a redundancy between the variables. The lack of relationships for high blue-collar respondents perhaps indicates that the high blue-collar do not join organizations that approve of or make them aware of the Urban League.

In general, the combined results for both Urban League and NAACP parallel very closely those found for each considered alone. Since analysis of CORE, SNCC, and the Black Muslims does not involve confusion of belonging and approving, the issues can be more clearly seen in such analysis.

CORE, SNCC, AND THE BLACK MUSLIMS

The three remaining Negro-rights organizations are widely known for their militancy and are distinguished by membership consistent with their purposes.[9] They have negligible membership in Tampa and may therefore be considered all together. In order to obtain clarity in presentation, one organization, SNCC, will be presented in detail.

In Table 19, the relationship of coracialism for each occupational status level is presented. White-collar respondents with high coracialism more often claim they would not join than do those with medium or low. The same result is obtained for the high blue-collar set (but the number of cases is quite small). By contrast, those with low coracialism would join, among both high blue-collar and low blue-collar workers.

Since the willingness to join other organizations proved

TABLE 19

CORACIALISM, OCCUPATIONAL STATUS, AND
ATTITUDES TO SNCC (PERCENTS)

CORACIALISM	Would join	Unde-cided	Would not join	Total %	(N)
White-collar					
High	15	28	57	100	87
Medium	11	43	46	100	28
Low	14	55	31	100	29
High blue-collar					
High	19	19	62	100	21
Medium	12	49	39	100	155
Low	20	40	40	100	82
Low blue-collar					
High	13	46	41	100	89
Medium	9	57	34	100	223
Low	8	49	43	100	177

to be relevant in analysis of the NAACP and Urban League,
it was studied in detail for SNCC also. We found that those
male low blue-collar workers who were members of one or
no voluntary associations were more likely to join SNCC
than those who belonged to two or more voluntary associations. This subset is quite small, however, and this finding
should be viewed with caution. In addition, low blue-collar
workers having high reinforcement more often say they
would not join SNCC than those with less reinforcement.
It would seem that unions are decisive among this set of
workers, and the unions seem to lean toward NAACP rather
than SNCC. It seems safe to conclude that opposition to

TABLE 20

CORRELATIONS OF ATTITUDES TO JOINING
AND SOCIAL RELATIONSHIPS:
SNCC, CORE, BLACK MUSLIMS

	White-collar	High blue-collar	Low blue-collar
SNCC			
Coracialism	High, would not join	High, would not join	High, would join Low, would not join
Reinforcement (males)	—	—	High, would not join
CORE			
Coracialism	—	High, would not join Medium, un-decided Low, would join	High, would join Medium, un-decided Low, would not join
Collegiality	—	—	High, would join
Black Muslims			
Coracialism	High, would not join	—	—
Reinforcement (males)	High, would not join	—	—

SNCC is rather widely distributed and sufficiently strong to obscure variations due to the amount of other memberships.

When the three organizations are considered separately for three status levels, three social relations variables, and males and females, there are fifty-four comparisons, and of these there are fourteen statistically significant results. Of these only three are positive correlations with joining, two of which regard low blue-collar interest in CORE. The results are listed in Table 20.

The coracialism and attitude findings regarding SNCC, CORE, and Black Muslims summarized in Table 20 are presented in detail (but without the occupation control) in Table 21. It can be seen that there is less variation in disapproval of CORE and the Muslims than of SNCC.

As in previous chapters concerned with joining only, collegiality again proves to be relatively unimportant as an independent variable. It lacks correlation with favorable attitudes toward membership in those voluntary associations with little local membership. In every instance where there is a correlation, albeit partially redundant, it is a positive one, i.e., the greater the collegiality, the more frequently respondents belong or are favorable toward membership in that voluntary association.

Reinforcement is also unimportant in generating opinions toward Negro-rights voluntary associations. As in the case of collegiality, reinforcement is not related to opinions of these voluntary associations among high blue-collar respondents. There is only one instance where reinforcement is important among the white-collar (CORE) and one instance among the blue-collar (SNCC).

We began this chapter with the observation that in earlier chapters a relationship had been found between actual Negro-rights voluntary association memberships and several of our independent variables concerning social relations at work. NAACP had the highest actual membership of all the Negro-rights voluntary associations. In this chapter we

TABLE 21

CORACIALISM AND ATTITUDES TO SNCC, CORE, AND BLACK MUSLIMS

CORACIALISM	Would join %	Unde-cided %	Would not join %	Total %	N
SNCC					
High	14.7	35.1	50.2	100	(197)
Medium	10.6	52.7	36.7	100	(406)
Low	12.2	46.8	41.0	100	(288)
CORE					
High	31.0	40.5	28.5	100	(200)
Medium	20.4	54.9	24.7	100	(417)
Low	22.6	50.7	26.7	100	(296)
Black Muslims					
High	2.5	15.4	82.1	100	(202)
Medium	4.0	21.2	74.8	100	(424)
Low	4.9	19.1	76.0	100	(304)

have found that Negroes apparently discriminate among Negro-rights associations in opinion as well as in actual membership, but that the social relations at work influence how Negroes feel about joining less than does occupational status.[10]

CHURCH MEMBERSHIP AND ATTITUDES

Variations in social-relationship variables show some correlation with attitudes toward joining Negro-rights voluntary

associations, but much less correlation than with membership itself. We have not, however, utilized the full range
of collateral materials that were found useful in explanation
of causes of membership. Exploration of the effects of church
membership seems indicated in this case, since the church
is explicitly concerned with values and attitudes and holds
a place of prominence in the Negro community.

Since we have shown that church membership and
church-related voluntary association membership is relatively
higher among low-status occupations than among voluntary
associations, we might expect lower-status respondents' attitudes toward voluntary associations to be differentiated by
whether or not they belong to a church. This proves to be
the case. When attitudes to joining the five organizations are
analyzed by occupational status and church vs. nonchurch,
the only significant concern with membership is among the
low blue-collar and not-working. The Black Muslims and
SNCC are rejected; the Urban League and the NAACP are
approved; and CORE, in between as usual, is significantly
often the object of indecision.

NOTES

1. Part of the reason for low attendance in Negro-rights
organizations (but high rates of approval of them, as we shall
see later) is their infrequent meetings. The principal organizations, NAACP, and the Urban League, are large and are governed
by boards that meet regularly. However, each has many func-
tioning committees that give members ample opportunities to
participate or hold minor offices. One of the writers has served

on committees of each and can testify to the chances they offer
for involvement. It may be that this kind of involvement is
attractive only to more educated people, which helps to account
for the class bias of the measured membership.

2. In this regard, see our discussion in chapter 1 on occupational communities. "Linkages" is a more general concept used
to refer to the captivity of members of voluntary associations.
From our research, two types of captivity emerge: those of direct
sponsorship by (or tolerance or accommodation to) a primary
association with stability and economic power; and those by a
secondary association related to the primary one and receiving
its livelihood from the primary one. Seymour M. Lipset, Martin
Trow, and J. S. Coleman described in *Union Democracy* an occupational community of our secondary type, in which the union
is the focus of voluntary associations of printers. We would
argue that this type is only pseudoextensive, in that its integrative aspects operate only among union members. An example
of the primary type would be athletic leagues within the aegis
of a large company. Little of this concerns Negroes, which fact
may ultimately promote their community integration. The most
prominent example of primary linkage is that of the teachers'
professional associations; if these in turn sponsored internal voluntary associations among teachers, they would be an occupational community.

3. The small number of those who join makes pursuit of
the problem fruitless. What needs explanation is not so much
the theory (involving coracialism, reinforcement, and collegiality)
but the larger issue of the nature of high blue-collar workers
that repeatedly appears to be crucial in understanding Negro
life. Some comments may be ventured in passing. Skilled workers
are the highest status set below the white-collar barrier, which
is typically breached in intergenerational rather than intragenera-
tional mobility. Skilled workers may find taking risks to be very
threatening. Negro skilled workers, frequently in the building
trades, are often isolated from the Negro community and their
unions give them little security. Negro semiskilled or operative

workers, although of a lower objective status, may in some cases have steadier work and the prestige of operating powerful machines. The most significant differences, for our research, between white and Negro high blue-collar workers, is that at least the whites' unions have got them something—some security, some bargaining power, and relatively higher incomes for wage work. Locally, Negroes have none of this and, apparently, they do not find that belonging to the NAACP is a way out, either.

4. This operationalism is not an intellectual commitment of the writers, but is, we believe, the level of meaning appropriate to this research.

5. The placement of the attitude questions within the interview can be determined by consulting the Interview Schedule in the Appendix.

6. Robin M. Williams, Jr., *Strangers Next Door: Ethnic Relations in American Communities,* p. 336.

7. The distinction between local and nonlocal Negro-rights organizations divides the organizations into two sets. It also is approximately coincident with a cleavage between the same organizations as to social class, in an unusual manner. We have pointed out the white-collar membership component of the Urban League and the NAACP. CORE and SNCC, on the other hand, generally have been differently composed, although it is not safe to make any simple class distinctions. CORE and SNCC have had a high proportion of prestatus members, such as those who have prepared for normal white-collar occupations but have not claimed them. Both have at times had mixtures of black and white youth, intellectuals, lower-class militants, and religious and political activists in various coalitions or mixes. The Black Muslims also tend to be lower class in constituency. Reasons for rejecting them locally may be due both to a defense of Christianity and a rejection of militance for a variety of reasons. But CORE, SNCC, and the Muslims have in common a general rejection of the prestige that characterizes the NAACP and Urban League. The fact that CORE and SNCC have not prospered in Tampa should not be ignored. The attitudes we find are thus simultaneously a product of the distance and strangeness of CORE and

SNCC and of the social conditions that are responsible for their absence.

8. When we say "more often" or "more likely" it must be remembered that we refer to more than expected under the null hypothesis.

9. We are measuring not militance, as Gary Marx did in *Protest and Prejudice,* but the approval of organizations. Even if his finding that higher class is related to higher militance is true for our sample, it would not necessarily contradict our findings. We are *assuming,* and not measuring, the militance of these organizations, which is another issue. We would argue that, in general, the NAACP and the Urban League are more conservative than CORE and SNCC, and the former have higher prestige and higher status members, but that comparative status is not the main issue. Rather, a large number of CORE and SNCC members are prestatus oriented (i.e., they have educational qualifications for statuses they have not claimed, or ascriptive statuses to which they have not matured) or they are deviants from typical occupational structures.

10. The findings are relevant to the recent shift in interest to accessible civil-rights efforts—to organizations that "reach the people." The NAACP apparently is *not* such an organization. The fact that it is centralized and bureaucratic suggests its essentially middle-class nature. Decentralized, small, intimate, "close to the people" units—gemeinschafts—are precisely those that are capable of having a lower-class appeal.

The actions of the NAACP may have led to development of other organizations because its method (centralization) left an "organizational gap" regarding the unattached masses that it could not reach. Our data support this position: the NAACP enjoys widespread favorable rating and far less membership—it has a very low favorable-opinion-to-membership ratio.

Thus the NAACP has experienced, perhaps, the dilemma of all associations: precisely as it achieves national eminence and power it loses in one sense its basis of support in the masses. Success generates the seeds of each new opposition in a Marxian dialectic.

6

CHURCH AND UNION: VITAL NONVOLUNTARY ASSOCIATIONS

In these later chapters we have set aside the causal analysis relating work and voluntary association membership for consideration of the relationships between multiple variables in a more complex scheme. Church and union are important parts of this approach: neither wholly cause nor caused in our analytic schema, they take on multiple values as parts of the complex wholes that are communities.

The two kinds of organizations have in common their less than voluntary membership. We should not be misled by this observation into treatment of them jointly, for as organizations they are quite different. Membership in a church, or acceptance of a faith, is heavily ascriptive and based on the continuity of family and community; membership in a union is not ascriptive nor wholly compulsory, but is a product of the nature of the conflict between employers and workers, which is contingent on the individual because he must work. We therefore must adopt an analytical strategy appropriate to each type of organization. For the church, our interest is in aspects of a uniquely Negro institution in the black community: who belongs and who does not, what types of churches exist and who belongs and to each type, and what is the relationship of each of these to voluntary association membership. The union has already been considered causally as a principal element in the reinforcement variable. Our attention therefore turns to the more descriptive aspect: who belongs to unions, what unions there are, what cognate things are true of union members, and what specific links there are between unions and voluntary associations. In brief, the issue is: what is the most significant thing about these two kinds of organizations for the study of voluntary associations in black communities?

THE CHURCH

Types of Churches

Two important axes of classification in religion are belief systems and types of organization.[1] Although the former is of importance in understanding religion of contemporary Negroes, much of the range of variation is automatically eliminated from consideration by the existential conditions of the research city. The central belief systems are overwhelmingly Protestant Christian, and although there are many doctrinal differences, the errors that would be introduced by attempting to classify them are greater than the error made by ignoring them. We shall, in fact, find ample justification for treating such contrasting belief systems as Roman Catholic and Episcopalian as a common set on the basis of their local organizational similarity, which obscures doctrinal differences. We shall lump Methodists and Baptists in a group on the same grounds. The basis of grouping is organizational similarity, not belief.

In classifying religious organizations we used a procedure similar to that employed in classifying voluntary associations. We had in mind a general theory about the types, and then we gathered information about churches from newspapers, informants, and personal participation. Our classification represents distinctions that the community makes, put into a limited number of sets for research purposes.

We found a number of people who attended church occasionally but did not belong and were not willing to specify any church preference. This set was labeled "no preference." The few Roman Catholics and Episcopalians are merged into one set. Methodists and Baptists are numerically large and have much similarity as to congregational autonomy, type of service, and internal structure. Extensive analysis of their social characteristics fails to reveal significant differences between them. Primitive Baptist and Missionary Baptist form another cluster, similar in type to what Yinger calls "the established sect."[2] They are intensely concerned with religious purity and are strongly fundamentalist. The last

TABLE 22

CHURCH MEMBERSHIP BY OCCUPATION AND SEX

| | CHURCH MEMBERSHIP PERCENTS | |
OCCUPATIONAL STATUS	Male	Female
White-collar	80.6	82.3
High blue-collar	61.6	66.7
Low blue-collar	65.0	78.8
Not working	52.9	74.4

group are similar to the cultic: highly individualistic, of usually small local units, and often characterized by such anti-scientific practices as faith healing. They are inherently unstable and often temporary organizations because they organize on the basis of beliefs that are essentially nonworldly.

For the sake of simplicity, these types may be called, respectively, "church" (Roman Catholic, Episcopal), denomination (Methodist, Baptist), established sect (Primitive Baptist, Missionary Baptist, Presbyterian mission, Mennonite mission), cult (miscellaneous local names). Whenever reference is made to "church," quotation marks will be used to preserve the distinction from church as a general inclusive category.

The membership in churches is tabulated for both males and females in Table 22. Two facts previously noted about the population should be mentioned. First, female respondents in the high blue-collar set are slightly underrepresented. Second, our sampling method was aimed at workers, and only secondarily was sex considered. As a consequence, female heads of household are probably overrepresented, which may make the data for women somewhat unreliable for purposes of comparison with all possible women in the sample area. In spite of these issues, there is a clear tendency for the women to exceed the men in church membership by a greater proportion as occupational status decreases.

Who Belongs to Churches?

Twenty-seven percent of the respondents do not claim church membership (no preference). The nonmembers, however, are not evenly distributed by occupation. The relationship between nonmembership and proportion of the sample is shown in Table 23. As can be seen from the two tables,

TABLE 23

CHURCH NONMEMBERSHIP BY OCCUPATION

OCCUPATIONAL STATUS	Percent of total nonmembers	Percent of occupational status
White-collar	8.9	13.8
High blue-collar	32.3	25.4
Low blue-collar	46.7	48.0
Not working	12.0	12.8
	99.9	100.0

[a] N = 1,072; no information from 14 respondents.

nonmembership is unevenly distributed, and the high blue-collar are heavily overrepresented.

The occupational distribution of membership in the

church types is presented in Table 24. By comparing the percent figures with the percent of total row at the bottom

TABLE 24

MEMBERSHIP IN EACH CHURCH TYPE BY
OCCUPATIONAL STATUS

OCCUPATIONAL STATUS	"Church" %	Denomination %	Established sect %	Cult %	Total %
White-collar	9.8	61.5	23.0	5.7	100.0
High blue-collar	3.4	54.2	38.5	3.9	100.0
Low blue-collar	2.1	57.9	35.5	4.5	100.0
Not working	3.9	60.8	25.5	9.8	100.0
N	(30)[a]	(453)	(257)	(41)	(781)
Percent of total sample	3.8	58.1	32.9	5.2	100.0

[a] Nonmembers excluded. Figures in parentheses refer to column totals.

of the table, the proportion of over- or under-representation may be visualized.[3] White-collar respondents are overrepresented in the "church," and slightly overrepresented in denomination and cults. High and low blue-collar workers are more evenly represented. The not-working set shows the largest variation, with underrepresentation in the established sect and overrepresentation in the cults.

Let us shift to another perspective: the identity of the members of religious organizations. There are some very definite status composition differences between types (see Table 25).[4] The "church" set emerges as the closest to a true white-collar organization type, while the remainder are heavily blue-collar by proportion. Two results run counter

TABLE 25

CHURCH MEMBERSHIP COMPOSITION
BY OCCUPATIONAL STATUS[a]

OCCUPATIONAL STATUS	"Church" %	Denomination %	Established sect %	Cult %	Total respondents %
White-collar	40.0	16.6	10.9	17.1	13.8
High blue-collar	20.0	21.4	26.9	17.1	25.4
Low blue-collar	26.7	48.3	52.1	41.4	48.0
Not working	13.3	13.7	10.1	24.4	12.8
	100.0	100.0	100.0	100.0	100.0
N	30	453	257	41	

[a] Nonmembers excluded.

to common expectations: the strong weighting of "church" toward white-collar, and the unexpected proportion of white-collar cult members. However, both the "church" and the cult numbers are small, and the perceived variations may not be adequate samples of the true distribution.

The material on the church presented to this point has some important implications regarding the theme of mass society vs. pluralist society, which has guided our research. The church is by far the most pervasive community social organization, joined by more people than are voluntary associations as a whole and providing a membership of some kind for a wider range of persons by age and social status than any other organization. This being the case, the church leadership offered by the most educated people measures community leadership as a whole, to an important degree.

Are the high-status people distributed where their influence can be felt? The white-collar workers are more often members than any other set, and both men and women are highly involved. When, however, we look at Table 25, we see that it is in the numerically largest categories, the denominations and the established sects, that the white-collar workers are lowest in proportion to the number of members. A further fact, which does not appear in the tables, exacerbates the problem considerably. By our observation, the white-collar workers predominate in the very large, prestigious churches of the denomination and established sect. Thus, the apparent distribution of respondents by status in the two sects is not reflected in a similar distribution in specific local churches. The quality of leadership is, of course, not evaluated in these comments.

The irony of the matter is increased when we realize that it is precisely the "church," which has the strongest hierarchical structure and authority and least needs high-status people to achieve its goals, that has the largest proportion of white-collar workers. The free church, for which voluntarism is so vital, has the smallest proportion of educated people.

If this analysis is essentially correct, it points to a self-defeating prophecy for the churches of black people. One of the reasons that people abandon churches is that the responsibility of leading and financing becomes too great. The high proportion of white-collar members in "church" and somewhat less in cult may be a response to the heavy burdens of leading the mass of the Negroes who belong to the denominations and established sects of the center. What has been said here is true in lesser degree for the churches of whites, because the status distribution of occupations among whites is more even; the numbers of businessmen, lower white-collar workers, and salaried skilled workers is larger; and the income and education of the working class is higher.

Two added measures help to interpret the findings: attendance data and subjective evaluation of friendship. Attendance at church can be measured somewhat more exactly than that of voluntary associations, since almost all churches meet weekly (at least) whereas voluntary associations are far more variable. Exact attendance data were tabulated from respondents' answers, and the results are categorized as "often," "sometimes," or "never."[5] The material is tabulated in Table 26, as "percent often," since the "sometimes" and "never" categories are relatively uniform and small throughout.[6] Considering the large range of variation encountered in voluntary associations, the differences by occupation and

TABLE 26

PERCENT WHO ATTEND CHURCH OFTEN
BY CHURCH TYPE AND OCCUPATIONAL STATUS[a]

OCCUPATIONAL STATUS	"Church" %	Denomination %	Established sect %	Cult %
White-collar	67.0[a]	77.5	77.0	100.0[a]
High blue-collar	0.0[a]	67.0	56.5	85.9
Low blue-collar	25.0[a]	66.3	67.5	69.6
Not working	50.0[a]	64.6	73.0	50.0
N	(30)	(453)	(231)	(66)
% N attending	40.0	68.0	66.3	74.2

[a] Total fewer than ten in cell.

TABLE 27

CHURCH FAMILIARITY BY CHURCH TYPE AND
OCCUPATIONAL STATUS (SUMMARY OF DATA)

PERCENT FAMILIAR WITH MOST IN ATTENDANCE

OCCUPATIONAL STATUS	No church preference %	"Church" %	Denomi- nation %	Established sect %	Cult %
White-collar	12.5	58.3	62.6	57.7	77.8[a]
High blue-collar	4.4	16.6[a]	53.1	45.2	64.2
Low blue-collar	13.6	37.5[a]	45.9	44.1	63.6
Not working	11.1	75.0[a]	50.8	65.3	70.0

[a] Fewer than ten in cell.

type are remarkably small. Following the white-collar category, there is a rise in attendance from "church" to cult. It is
apparently unrelated to proportion of white-collar members
of the category. In addition, the results do not confirm the
typical finding of higher attendance of Catholics than Protestants (the "church" category of course includes Episcopalians
as well). Outside of the uniform higher attendance of white-
collar members, there is little variation in attendance by occupation where there are large enough numbers of cases to
consider.

Respondents were asked about what proportion of people they recognized the last time they attended church
("church familiarity"). We would expect the results to be
less reliable among those who had not recently attended,
but since attendance rates are relatively even in distribution
the error is probably distributed uniformly at least in the

larger cells. The data are summarized in Table 27 (full data in Table 28). For the whole sample, church familiarity is significantly higher with higher occupational status.

In general, however, the church familiarity differences between church types are more striking than the differences between occupational statuses. Predictably, nonmembers have a very low familiarity score. Cult members are uniformly higher than other types, in each occupational status set.

It is generally true for the whole sample that the smaller congregations are found in churches attended by lower-status people. This fact helps to explain the higher church familiarity rates of the not-working than the blue-collar. However, there is no reason to assume smaller con-

TABLE 28

CHURCH FAMILIARITY BY CHURCH TYPE AND
OCCUPATIONAL STATUS (COMPLETE DATA)

OCCUPATIONAL STATUS	Familiarity response	No church prefer-ence	"Church"	De-nomina-tion	Estab-lished sect	Cult
White-collar	most	3	7	47	15	7
	half	7	4	23	10	2
	none	14	1	5	1	0
High blue-collar	most	4	1	52	28	9
	half	29	1	36	27	2
	none	58	4	10	7	3
Low blue-collar	most	18	3	100	52	21
	half	27	4	89	45	6
	none	87	1	29	21	6
Not working	most	4	3	31	17	7
	half	8	0	21	5	1
	none	24	1	9	4	2

gregational size among higher-status cult members than
lower-status cult members—all of them would be small.
Therefore, the high proportion of familiarity and attendance
of white-collar cultists is understandable and remarkable.

Now we may add observations about attendance patterns to the commentary previously made about the meaning
of membership patterns. The highest rate of attendance
claimed is that of the white-collar workers in denomination
and established sect (except cult, with a small number of
cases). These are the organizations in which, it was claimed,
white-collar members are concentrated as a status set but
lowest as a proportion of the religious organization type.
Whether this indicates strong responsibility and leadership
or high attendance at key prestige churches and less responsibility for the whole community is a matter of speculation.

The high blue-collar set is the most overrepresented
(see Table 24) in the established sect, yet when attendance
is considered in that category, it has the poorest record. The
irregular attendance of the high blue-collar set is marked
throughout. Without further information about size of congregation, it is not feasible to proceed with more detailed
interpretation.

What can be concluded from the membership, attendance, and familiarity data considered jointly? The most
striking findings are among the white-collar workers, who
form larger than expected proportions of "church" and cult.
They attend "church" somewhat less frequently, cult more
frequently, and in similar proportion, they feel familiar less
often with "church" and more often with cult members. There
are, then, two deviant or contrary-to-stereotype small groups

of white-collar workers who are distinctly different from each other, and a very large contingent in denomination and established sect types.

Now that some of the characteristics of the church and occupational status have been outlined, it is possible to proceed to the relationship of membership in church types and voluntary associations.

Church and Voluntary Association Membership

The patterns of voluntary association and church membership are presented in detail in Table 29.

The white-collar workers now appear to have certain unique characteristics in addition to those already noted, with the few "church" members having high voluntary association rates and the cult members having low rates.[7] White-collar cult members are few and highly involved, know nearly everyone in a (probably) small congregation, attend often, and specialize (see chapter 4 regarding this concept). White-collar "church" members, on the other hand, follow the pattern typical of other white-collar workers in secular matters, but with a lower church attendance rate and wider voluntary association participation. On the whole, Negro Catholics are among the most Protestant-like of all.

High rates of voluntary association membership, typical of white-collar workers in general, are concentrated in the two largest categories, the denomination and the established sect. Membership in denomination and established sect are also associated with relatively higher rates of participation in voluntary associations regardless of occupation.

In general, church and voluntary association membership is correlated. Higher status means higher membership.

TABLE 29

VOLUNTARY ASSOCIATION MEMBERSHIP,
CHURCH MEMBERSHIP, AND CHURCH TYPE
BY OCCUPATIONAL STATUS

OCCUPATIONAL STATUS AND VOLUNTARY ASSOCIATION MEMBERSHIP	No prefer- ence	"Church"	De- nomina- tion	Estab- lished sect	Cult
White-collar					
0	13	4	16	4	5
1	5	1	15	5	1
2+	8	7	44	18	3
High blue-collar					
0	76	4	40	28	5
1	14	2	30	17	7
2+	4	0	27	17	2
Low blue-collar					
0	116	3	116	65	17
1	14	2	55	30	10
2+	6	3	48	23	6
Not working					
0	30	2	34	15	8
1	6	0	12	6	2
2+	1	2	16	5	1
Total	293	30	453	233	67

Although classifying churches as nonvoluntary associations
is justified on the frequently cited grounds of stronger expectations (typically complied with) for church membership, the overall membership patterns are quite similar, except for higher participation of lower-status workers in religious than in secular organizations.

We pointed out in chapter 2 that it is sometimes difficult to make a clear distinction between operating parts of the church and church-related voluntary associations. The strength of the ties between church and church-related organizations is reflected in a second measure: a strong association between church attendance and church-related organization membership at each status level.

The voluntary association membership rates of those who do not participate in church are generally low, with a net of 26.1 percent. The issue is not simply that of a choice between sacred and profane organizational outlets for personal interests. What we find is a tendency for church nonmembers to be nonparticipants in voluntary associations as well. Compare, for example, the sharp differences by occupational status between church nonmembers and members of denominations and established sects. The distinction even holds for the not-working.

Religious Membership and Type of Voluntary Association Membership

Having traced who belongs to churches, to what kind of churches, and members' feelings of familiarity in churches, we now turn to the relationship between church membership and types of voluntary association.

The expected strong relation between church membership and church-related voluntary associations was found. Religious membership was significantly related to the membership in regular lodges for low blue-collar workers and to mutual-aid lodges for high blue-collar. Several other facts reinforce the assumption of a membership link between lodges and churches. Church familiarity was significantly correlated with membership in regular lodges for blue-collar workers, as well as for the not-working. It was found that members of established sects were more often regular lodge members than were members of any other church type. White-collar workers who belonged to denominations were frequently members of each kind of lodge, but there was no relation for the white-collar set as a whole. Although the pattern is somewhat irregular, perhaps caused by the irregular pattern of social-relations variables themselves, the general tendency to institutional membership covariation is clear. This conclusion is highlighted by a negative finding: "church" members do not participate, perhaps because of the lack of Catholic lodges for Negroes, and cult members do not participate, for reasons that are not readily apparent.

Lodges are neither left nor right in the Negro community, but are middle Protestant, and the church ties are quite strong. Apparently the strength of the white-collar leadership in mutual-aid lodges is related to the fact that the president of the largest lodge, a prominent businessman, is also a leading member of his denomination. Regular lodges are not similarly led.

Since we found that differences in church membership were characteristic of men and women, and that there were also differences in their voluntary association membership, it is important to check for covariation of these differences. Accordingly, the foregoing relations between church membership and voluntary associations were analyzed for males only. None of the results changes sufficiently to alter the statistical significance of the previous conclusions.

We find no reason to assume a tie between church and PTA similar to that between church and lodge. Nevertheless, there are correlations between white-collar "church," denomination, and established sect memberships and PTA membership rates. In chapter 4 we traced the relationship of white-collar teachers, professional voluntary associations, and PTA membership. What we probably have here is the fact that public school teachers are proportionately distributed among "church," denomination, and established sects, but apparently are less often found in cults and among those who have no church preference.

One type of voluntary association is characterized by uniform lack of correlation with church membership. There is no positive statistical correlation between church membership and social club membership, nor between church attendance and social club membership. Examination of the data shows an apparently strong cleavage between the two. Church familiarity of white-collar workers was associated with their social club membership—common friendships or similar orientations to friendship may be involved. White-collar workers were found, in chapter 4, to be the most frequent social club members.

Church membership is associated with membership in professional voluntary associations, but when analyzed by sex, this result does not hold for men.

Religious Membership and Negro-Rights Voluntary Associations

Membership in Negro-rights organizations as a whole was related to church membership only among white-collar workers. It was found in chapter 4 that Negro-rights voluntary associations were strong in white-collar membership. As among PTA members, white-collar Negro-rights membership was distributed among church types rather evenly.

There was one exception to the white-collar membership pattern. Low blue-collar church attendance and church familiarity was correlated with membership in Negro-rights organizations.

When the different types of Negro-rights organizations were considered separately, it was seen that low blue-collar membership in the NAACP was related to church membership, but membership in the Urban League was not. Church familiarity was also related to low blue-collar membership in the NAACP, and to membership in the Urban League, as well. It must be recalled that the proportion of low blue-collar workers who belonged to either the NAACP or the Urban League was small, and a considerable part were males who belonged to a union (i.e., high reinforcement). Why union and church membership should covary with NAACP membership is not clear, since there is no evidence of a relationship between church and union.

In chapter 5, attitudes to Negro-rights organizations were examined in detail. When these evaluations of SNCC, CORE, and Black Muslims are tabulated with church membership, it is again the low blue-collar set that proves to be the most interesting. Low blue-collar church membership was correlated with rejection of SNCC and the Muslims, while church members of all occupational status sets were essentially indifferent to CORE. Low blue-collar church familiarity patterns were identical to membership patterns as to rejection of SNCC and Muslims and similarly undecided about CORE. The low blue-collar rejection of radical Negro-rights organizations seems to be reciprocal with its acceptance of Urban League and NAACP, for both church members and nonmembers.

These findings about church and Negro-rights organizations should not be misconstrued. The most consistent finding is that a great many Negroes are simply indifferent to Negro-rights organizations.

THE UNION

The union is the second of the two nonvoluntary associations, that we shall consider, that has a sizable adult membership in the Negro community. Throughout the book we have made observations about unions, which may be summarized briefly by way of introduction.

Unions are voluntaristic in one sense. They represent an attempt by workers to further their own interests and the interests of other workers. Many unions have supplementary interests like those of voluntary associations, including political action, welfare or charity, recreation or sports, and so on. Some unions sponsor voluntary associations among their own members, or their members participate in voluntary associations as union members.

On the other hand, the ordinary union member encounters the union in a very nonvoluntary aspect. The union typically is in conflict with an employer, frequently quite openly. Its survival depends on organizing workers, which may mean competing with companies for workers' loyalty by all possible means. The worker encounters the union in this aspect, and not as a voluntary association that he may join at his pleasure.

The community expectation that a person will join a

church gives the church a certain nonvoluntary characteristic, but this is a very different sort of norm from that related to joining unions. The source of the church-joining norm is traditional, supplemented by interests related to that tradition. The source of the union-joining norm is prudence and the need for power, developed out of economic necessity. It is no surprise, then, that church-joining is diffused widely in society, but union-joining is particularistic, found only where the organization of the economy and the workers make it possible and necessary.

The union was used in chapters 2 and 4 as a research variable, as the major component of the reinforcement index. We found that reinforcement was only irregularly related to voluntary association membership for each occupational status because of the unbalanced distribution of the categories of workers who were unionized. Where a concentration of workers was found and where unions were also concentrated, there seemed to be a strong effect on voluntary association membership. A major proportion of the discussion that follows is oriented to this problem: who is unionized, and what is their social identity?

Union Membership

Almost 15 percent of the respondents belonged to a union. They were, however, not evenly distributed by occupational status. There were very few union members among the white-collar or those not working. The latter suggests that unions have some success in maintaining employment for their members, and this is important for our research. To put it in research terms, union nonmembers appear in either the low blue-collar category or the not-working category by chance alone a large proportion of the time, because of the irregular nature of employment and because of the chance that the interview occurred between jobs. This is not true, however, for union workers who only rarely appear as "not-working." Union membership, therefore, distinguishes the population of our low blue-collar category into specific subpopulations, but does not distinguish the not-working.

Some of the variations in union membership have to do with different rates of union membership of males and females. Comparative data are presented in Table 30.

There are only two female union members in the entire blue-collar group, out of 221 in the category. Because of the small number of high blue-collar women who appear in the sample, it is not possible to ascertain whether the small number of union members found among them represents the actual situation. Perhaps greater importance should be attached to the fact that there were so few because in high blue-collar families, men were more often heads of

TABLE 30

UNION MEMBERSHIP BY OCCUPATIONAL
STATUS AND SEX (PERCENTS)

OCCUPATIONAL STATUS	Male	Female
High blue-collar	18.8(250)[a]	4.0(25)
Low blue-collar	28.6(332)	—(186)
Total	24.4(582)	1.0(211)

[a] Figures in parentheses refer to number of cases in the base.

families and thus appear in the sample relatively more often
than women.

The union represents a major common membership
for the low blue-collar workers. The only thing they join
more often is the church. Looked at in another sense, they
belong to voluntary associations less often than do those of
higher status; they belong to churches less often (except
some specific types); but they belong to unions more often.
Characterized in terms of some sociological variables, their
memberships are specifically more involved in highly normative and coercive associations, and less in those oriented to
voluntarism and shared values.

Unions try to organize large proportions of the workers of any one employer. That is their ultimate source of
power. Unions are frequently irrelevant to isolated workers.
Unions are found most often among those whom we have
called company-employed, and these tend to be the larger
units of workers. In the research city, there are very few
industries where unions gain major victories for large numbers of Negro workers. This diffuseness of Negro labor and
the union power that supports it is reflected in the generally
weak correlation of union membership with our other variables. Black unions are weak, and their influence does not
show in the available measures.

When the correlation of union membership with voluntary association membership is studied for blue-collar
males, the only relationships are for high blue-collar with
joining Negro-rights organizations, especially the NAACP.
There is also a relationship of union membership and rejection of SNCC among the low blue-collar, a frequent kind
of finding in this research.

Of perhaps greater significance is a negative result: belonging to a union is not related to belonging to instrumental organizations for either blue-collar set. Unions do not have this kind of consequence in regard to intentional social change, so far as the available measures reveal. If they have any effect, it is in specific concentrations of relatively large numbers of Negro males, and those are very few in Tampa.

NOTES

1. The two systems are rarely used together. For a review of classification by organization type, see J. Milton Yinger, *Religion, Society, and the Individual.* For classification by belief systems, see Bryon Wilson, "An Analysis of Sect Development," *American Sociological Review* 24: 3–15.

2. Wilson, "Analysis of Sect Development."

3. This method of presentation is adopted in this chapter rather than the inferential statistical method that was used in chapters 2–5 because here we are not testing hypotheses.

4. Note that we are talking about numbers in a type, rather than the size of congregations of a type. The latter may vary within the type. The analysis would be sharpened considerably if the size of congregation were known. Experience has shown that accurate information of this kind is difficult to obtain.

5. The exact categories were: once per week or more; two or three times per month; once per month; less than once per month; never attends.

6. The overall weekly attendance rate, including "no preference" was 25.2 percent. We can find no comparable studies for cities in this region. Lenski reports a weekly attendance rate for Negro Protestants in Detroit of nearly 40 percent, and only 5

percent who never attend, compared to almost 8 percent in Tampa. He also notes, from Orbach, that Negro Catholics had attendance patterns similar to Negro Protestants, which is not true of the comparison of white Catholics and Protestants. Our findings are even more differentiated, with Negro Catholics (and Episcopalians, one-third of the category) with even less attendance than Protestants. Part of the difference may be due to the recency of Catholicism to southern Negroes, who still encounter partial segregation in Catholic churches (Gerhard Lenski, *The Religious Factor,* p. 40).

7. There is a partial redundancy in the data, since church members constitute the major source of members in church-related voluntary associations, which is a large voluntary association category. With the church-related voluntary associations eliminated, the differences are less striking but the main conclusions are not changed. Since the "church" members have few church-related memberships, their high proportion of voluntary associations is not altered by redundancy as much as members of the denomination and established sect sets.

7

RIOT
AND
ROUTINE

The field research for the final phase of this study began
in early May 1967. It was our intention to conduct
the field work in a short period of time with a relatively
large number of identically trained interviewers, in order to
diminish the effect of community change on opinion items
in the research schedule. The interviewing was to be completed before the end of the school year in mid-June, so that
changing conditions in the labor market would not intervene.

On Sunday, June 11, when about 80 percent of the
interviewing was completed, a major riot broke out in the

city, following the killing of a Negro youth during an arrest attempt by a white policeman. We had two field administrative centers in Negro communities, one of which was in a commercial zone about five blocks from the edge of the area where the riot began, and the second of which was in the center of what became the secondary riot area. Because of the location of these centers, it was decided to suspend interviewing until the safety of personnel could be assured. It was then decided that the interview schedules would not be rewritten to include questions relevant to the riot, in order to maintain the absolute identity of pre- and postriot schedules.

We anticipated that those questions that concerned opinions or attitudes toward voluntary associations or personal matters might be changed by the riot, but that structural or simply factual items would not. We therefore were presented with the opportunity to conduct a field experiment, with before-after changes to be expected in certain items due to the riot.

The experimental design is rare in sociology. It requires the existence in real communities of conditions that are difficult to create even in the laboratory. To illustrate, let us consider the hypothetical conditions of a simple before-after field experiment. Let us assume the existence of two cities that are identical in every respect, but that are independent of each other and do not interact over a period of a year. Then let us assume the introduction of an experimental factor in one city only, say a change in the educational system. At the end of the year, during which no other differentials are introduced between the cities, the change in one is completed and the resulting differences observed in relevant social variables are said to be due to the innovation. Obviously any attempt at such a design involves either control, which cannot be tolerated or practiced without unacceptable consequences, or more typically, unwarranted assumptions about experimental conditions. When small-group research is attempted in a clinical setting, an approximation to adequate control may sometimes be realized, but then another problem arises, namely that of generalizing the results to field conditions.

The design that was utilized in our research was forced upon us. It admitted of few options. First, there were no control cities. The city in which the riot took place had to serve as its own control. We were forced to assume that the things that are different after the riot have changed because of the riot alone. This assumption cannot take the standing of a proof because there was no other city in which we gathered data that could serve as a control. However, a second design feature allows some inferences about the causal properties of the riot. We gathered identical information in each of the six communities or distinct Negro residential areas, comprised of nineteen census tracts, and we can "hold constant" many of the demographic characteristics and variables of these areas and consider the inferences or implications of each of them before and after the riot. We can, therefore, with adequate qualifications, consider the research as a field experiment having moderately strong inferential properties. The chapter, then, has two significant features. It is rare that riots are researched adequately, and most riots are studies by evaluative or after-only designs. We therefore have a more valid reading on a riot than has previously appeared in sociological literature. Second, we are in a posi-

tion to explore the use of a methodological device that is
common in other sciences but is rare in sociology; the field
experiment. Somewhat more than previously, we try to use
completely the available materials, examining the relevance
of measures that would not be considered adequate in previous chapters where the research problem was under control
and not subject to exigencies.

We are not dealing with the problems that were of
concern to the Kerner commission. That is, we do not ask
why the riot started in one community and not another,
or why in Tampa and not, say, neighboring St. Petersburg.
Our focus is only on the riot, not on its causes or its implications. Nor do we consider directly whether the conditions that led to the riot themselves affected our variables.
In short, we have isolated a very specific problem: what
effect did a riot have on some specific opinion items relating to membership in voluntary associations? We believe the
design conditions are adequate to lead to some important
conclusions on this score.

This is not a study of before and after interviews of
the same people, but a comparison of samples gathered
before and after the riot. Consequently, differences between
the pre- and postriot samples are inferential as to changes
occurring over time in a given cohort of individuals. Considerable caution must be used in relation to the assumption
we make that the pre- and postriot samples are independent
random samples. On the other hand, the method has the
advantage that it is not necessary to rely on recollections
that respondents have of their preriot experiences or opinions,
as is necessary in after-only studies, nor do we encounter
the problem of contamination of data, which occurs in

before-after or panel studies repeatedly using the same respondent. In this chapter we will present major items of data in before-after form and attempt to explain the findings. But since the explanation involves specific features of the research city and the riot setting that have not been presented in preceding chapters, let us digress briefly to set the scene.

THE RIOT SETTING

Tampa is the third largest city in Florida. In 1960 it had a population of 274,970, which made it the 48th largest city in the U.S. At that time the nonwhite population was 46,456, or 16.9 percent of the total. The population per square mile was 3,235, which made it 108th among the 130 U.S. cities of 100,000 or more. Tampa ranks 51st from the highest of these cities in percent of nonwhite population. Tampa more than doubled its size in the decade between 1950 and 1960, and its rapid growth has continued.[1]

Tampa frequently has been characterized by its spokesmen as a city with relatively good race relations. Given the public relations consciousness of Floridians, we would expect such publicity. But Tampa could point to some notable accomplishments: school integration proceeded without major incident and more rapidly than was the case in most southern cities; before 1967 there had been no major race riots; advances were being made in jobs for Negroes; a biracial committee had functioned for many years and had some specific achievements to its credit. Throughout the year preceding the riot, community leaders, both Negro and white, showed cautious optimism about the possibility of avoiding "a Watts." In the few months preceding the outbreak, there was less reason for optimism, as several incidents involving police and Negroes approached the crisis level. These early incidents took place in the vicinity of what became the secondary riot area.

Tampa's Negro leaders—at least those most frequently consulted and cited—have been relatively moderate. There had been no large organized demonstrations, and the more militant civil-rights organizations such as CORE, SNCC, and SCLC had never gained a foothold. A small CORE group was organized, and a small mosque of the Temple of Islamic Science (Black Muslims) had existed for about two years.

THE RIOT

On the night of June 11 three Negro youths were alleged to have broken into a store on the edge of the central business district, adjacent to a Negro ghetto. They were pursued by police. One of them ran in the direction of his home and finally was shot by a white officer in an area adjacent to a small business district catering to Negroes, near a public housing project. The youth died en route to the hospital. A crowd quickly gathered and rumor spread that the killing was unjustified.

The news coverage of the event was extensive, both locally and nationally, and featured known leaders rather heavily. Since our research schedule had questions about five

Negro-rights organizations, it is important to estimate the extent to which each of them was featured. The only one mentioned prominently was the NAACP and this largely through its president. Other Negro leaders were mentioned simply as individuals or in their official status (e.g., high-school coach, biracial commission executive, minister, and the like). The NAACP might therefore be expected to be salient for postriot respondents, but other organizations would be evaluated much more indirectly.

White persons prominent in news media were the mayor, the sheriff, the chief of police, the governor, a white motorist saved from the rioters by a Negro, and specific policemen involved in the original incident.[2]

RESEARCH METHOD

Comments made about methodology in chapter 1 are applicable here, with the following minor additions. Interviewing was scheduled to achieve the maximum convenience and economy. Therefore, when the riot occurred, completed work was not distributed evenly over the entire area. Pre- and postriot samples are not necessarily random subsamples. In order to ascertain whether the deviation from randomness was within tolerable limits, we classified the interviews by census tract and tested (chi-square) for deviation from expected pre- and postriot frequency of interviews and for variation in major control factors such as occupation, sex, home ownership, age, length of residence, and rural background. The only significant deviation was slight underrepresentation of female high blue-collar workers in the riot area.

There were 876 preriot and 189 postriot interviews, of which 64 took place the first week following the riot, 44 the second, and 81 in the following month. Twenty-one other interviews were attempted before the riot but were sent back after the riot for completion of one or more items and were not included in the riot analysis. Since the interviews extended into the period of school summer vacation in which changes in the labor market might be expected, the major schedule items were extensively analyzed according to time elapsed from the riot. For the most part, we found no variation.

WHAT IS A RIOT?

Before proceeding to our findings, it might be helpful to point out some of the features of riots that are relevant to the variables under consideration. These comments form the basis for our attempt to explain our data.

Riots are spatially confined. They stop somewhere. Although the ability to maintain action requires a certain concentration of people, and this is limited by the distance from the source of the riot incident, the area in which rioting occurs seems to have an identity and a boundary so far as the parties to the riot are concerned. Negroes riot (recently) only where they are concentrated, and we know of no case where they have sustained action in territory identified as "white," or at a great distance from the riot origin, say, across open space between cities.

Riots are temporally confined. They involve mutual stimulation of persons to a pitch of excitement that cannot be maintained over long periods. Routinization and formalization always come, sooner or later, unless the riot is quickly suppressed by force. Most of the recent riots seem to go through a relatively predictable set of social stages (considering rioters only): triggering incident, crowd forming and excitement mounting, daring action and destruction (arson, looting). Then come many variations, depending on the response of police, leading to the denouement. Socially, rioting proceeds from crowd action to semipurposeful action, where daring opposition against police and violence to property have a purposeful aspect related to short-term plans and immediate goals, such as stealing specific available things, shooting a policeman or soldier who just happens to be accessible, or more rationally, stealing something related to plans for subsequent action. From the perspective of the police and civic authorities the paramount goal is always reestablishment of control, even where certain other values such as property and life need to be sacrificed in the process.

Riots are multisystemic. They become a fresh point of synthesis of all operative system levels of community life. For a short time, those closest to centers of action are totally mobilized personally, but never socially or culturally. Routine patterns of life are suspended or superseded, and the intricate patterns of norms and values that regulate life in reference to past and future are set aside for new priorities relating only to the present. In a riot, new values and new norms arise out of the immediate contacts of the fresh collective. Among the patterns set aside are those relating to self-gratification during leisure and those relating to plans for the future activities of community collectivities. By these phrases we have simply identified important aspects of expressive and instrumental voluntary associations. Leisure and plans are meaningless in a riot, when only action has significance. (We arbitrarily set aside the stimulating thought that rioting has become one of America's favorite leisure activities—Abbie Hoffman's *Revolution for the Hell of It* is a concept of this genre). Since superior power is in the hands of whites, control is soon established by them, and then routine voluntary associations may again meet at their leisure.

A riot transcends the social order. When social order is conceptualized in terms of some dichotomy like *gemeinschaft* and *gesellschaft,* or communal and associational, there is no place in it for phenomena like riots. A riot is neither communal nor associational because it is not of the social order in the conventional sense of that term; but both forms of order are reasserted in an attempt to end the destructiveness of the riot. The communal and associational forms of order, which we have considered to have causal impact on voluntary association membership, are suspended in different degrees during a riot. Work is appropriately altered to deal with contingencies. Unions attempt to assert their influence. Churches make appeals to moral principles. Informal social relations are altered in innumerable ways. As each germane collectivity reacts to the issues in relation to its own unique structure, order is reestablished and routine may ensue.

Interaction with Whites

The respondents in the postriot sample, significantly more frequently than in the preriot sample, reported that they "talked with *white* fellow employees" (for those who had white fellow employees). In Table 31 the results are presented in detail. Background data on talk with whites are presented in Appendix B, Table 43. Contrary to the commonplace assumption that riots produce or exacerbate Negro-white cleavages, the immediate consequence of the riot was an increase in interaction in those settings where Negroes

TABLE 31

"TALKS WITH WHITE FELLOW WORKERS"
BY TIME OF INTERVIEW

	TIME OF INTERVIEW	
TALKS WITH WHITE FELLOW WORKERS	Preriot %	Postriot %
Never	13.5	10.5
Some	60.4	42.9
Often	26.1	46.6
Total	100.0	100.0
N[a]	525	133

[a] Out of 1,065 total, 658 respondents reported having white fellow workers.

and whites interact as part of the daily activities of the community. This may, of course, simply reflect the desire of whites to be filled in on "the action." Such Negro-white interaction usually takes place in a setting dominated by whites. It also may be that the interest shown by whites (assuming that they initiate the contacts) is because the riot took place in the Negro community, and talking to a Negro coworker is the only way of getting a personal account of the action. In any event, the two-step communication thesis, which assumes that lower-status persons in a flow sequence pay attention to the higher-status source, is modified here when the lower-status Negro suddenly becomes the topic and source of communication.[3] Where Negroes are a potential threat group at work, the result might be different. But most southern whites are too secure in a segregated society to be seriously threatened by this kind of news.

It is also likely that in one sense the Negro communicator acts as a gatekeeper. Since he is an interpreter of a social world largely unknown to whites, and since there is little likelihood of feedback to check his interpretation, he is in a position to say only what he wants to have heard. He can edit the news to cope with his perceived social situation. This is highly favorable to him and may account for the fact that the riot appears to have had no negative consequences for his race-related personal contacts. To the Negro who works among whites there is a necessity to project a definition of the situation in which both races agree that "they" are rioting.

We contrast this with the civil-rights demonstrations, which often were accessible to whites since they typically took place in white or racially mixed places. The cordoning off of the riot area also reduced accessibility.

Interaction with Negroes

Not all types of interaction increased following the riot. There was a significant decrease in the proportion of respondents who reported that they talked at least "some" with their fellow employees (probably all Negro) when away from work (see Table 32). We are not sure how to

TABLE 32

"TALKS WITH FELLOW WORKERS AWAY FROM WORK" BY TIME OF INTERVIEW

TALKS WITH FELLOW WORKERS AWAY FROM WORK	TIME OF INTERVIEW	
	Preriot %	Postriot %
Never	25.9	38.4
Some	51.8	39.0
Often	22.3	22.6
Total	100.0	100.0
N[a]	753	164

[a] Of the 1,065 respondents, 917 had fellow workers.

interpret this. Perhaps there was a general withdrawal of Negroes from interaction with their Negro friends. There even may have been a general retrenchment of interaction within the Negro community, or a temporary decrease in the operation of extrafamilial groups. Three other questions

enabled us to check this possibility: the frequency of visiting friends and relatives (without regard to work relationships); more tenuously, the frequency of church attendance;
and the number of persons known the last time church was
attended.

The frequency with which respondents claim they
visited friends and relatives is no less among those interviewed following the riot than among those before the riot
(data not shown). If community interaction among Negroes
was curtailed following the riot, this must have taken place
for relationships other than "friends and relatives." Associat-
ing with fellow employees away from work probably was
curtailed because it involved travel away from the immediate neighborhood, and such travel is less often necessary
when visiting friends. In addition, an unknown proportion of
interaction off the job with fellow workers takes place in
bars, stores, or on streets near work, many of which were
inaccessible soon after the riot.

On the other hand, the church is traditionally an important organization in Negro life and its values should
be salient in a time of crisis. Accordingly, we would expect
the church to serve as a rallying point after the riot, independent of work and other community-related interaction.
Church membership, however, did not increase after the riot,
although we would be surprised if it changed much, since
it was so high to begin with.[4] The only change after the
riot was a reported decrease in attendance among low blue-
collar workers living farthest from the riot area.

Apparently, then, there was a selective but not a general retrenchment of interaction following the riot. Looked
at in another way, it takes something more than a killing,

the National Guard, and civil chaos to inspire these masses to go to church!

Inference from responses to another question allows a partial explanation. Those low blue-collar workers in the riot area who attend church frequently more often perceived the church to be filled with strangers after the riot than before. This suggests the strangers might be those who otherwise rarely attend, or that the riot situation altered perceptions of visitors. Also, the numbers attending might have been similar, but the composition of the group could have changed. It should be pointed out that our question inquired about familiarity "the last time" the respondent attended, which may not have been soon after the riot. The unavoidably inappropriate nature of the question perhaps obscures added variations that probably took place.

The Consequences of Interaction

We would expect increased interaction with whites to produce changes in attitudes to them, either positive or negative, and the minor changes in interaction with Negroes to lead to little change.[5] If this reasoning about the relations in the place of work holds true, we would expect an improvement in Negro-white relations, unless Negroes and whites are pitted against each other in the work situation for other reasons. This argument finds some support: the proportion of respondents who reported that white coworkers were very prejudiced was 6.6 percent before the riot and 1.4 percent after it.

Reasoning in similar fashion, if interaction among Negroes does not increase, no change in related sentiments and activities should be found. Two partial tests of this hypothesis can be made. Satisfaction with work did not change after the riot (although satisfaction at work would not be expected to be sensitive to this factor alone). Personal happiness (again, only a partial measure) likewise did not change. Background data on happiness and work satisfaction is presented in Appendix B, Tables 41 and 42.

Organizational Participation

Participation in organizations also might be related to the riot and to the impact of the riot on interaction.

Feagin found, in research on attitudes to violence following the Bedford-Stuyvesant riots of 1964, that Negroes who belonged to one or more organizations (other than church) were slightly more likely to advocate violence instead of nonviolence, while church members showed a reverse tendency.[6] The correlations were not strong, however. His study was post hoc, and the minor variations he found would lead us to expect only minor changes in our findings.

Organization membership is, of course, related to other sources of interaction as well, and to such factors as norms and values of the organizations, influence of mass media, participation in crowds, and so forth.

When total organizational memberships were considered, regardless of type, the only postriot change was among low blue-collar workers living away from the riot area: there was a strong increase in those who belonged to no organizations. We cannot explain this by any of the reasoning advanced so far. It may be noted that this change is consistent with the reported decrease in church attendance for the same respondents.

Attitudes to Organizations

In chapter 4 we examined the pattern of relationship between occupational status, a number of social variables, and support of various Negro-rights organizations. Because of the smaller number of cases in the postriot sample, full use cannot be made of each finding in a before-after comparison. In general, we proceed under the assumption that organizations known to be concerned with issues that were important during the riot might be expected to be more sensitive to the impact of the riot. Data on attitude change is presented in Table 33. The organization most likely to be evaluated differently following the riot is the NAACP, since it was so prominently involved in the Negro community. A substantial proportion belong to it (about 10 percent, more than any other Negro-rights organization) and a large proportion of Negroes express support for it whether or not they belong. But, as with the church, claimed membership in the NAACP does not increase significantly after the riot. Since the NAACP received a great deal of commendation and respect in the mass media during the riot, we might expect an increase in approval of it, independent of the interaction thesis. There was, however, no increase in approval, either the hypothetical approval (by the respondent himself) or respondent's report of perceived approval by fellow workers. There was only a small increase in neutrality toward the NAACP in the riot areas. This last observation fails to confirm the alleged widespread disenchantment with the NAACP among those living in riot areas, although it should be remembered that we did not interview the people allegedly most disenchanted—unmarried youth under twenty.

TABLE 33

PERCENT FAVORABLE TO NEGRO-RIGHTS
ORGANIZATIONS, PRERIOT AND POSTRIOT[a]

		White-collar	High blue-collar	Low blue-collar	Not-working
Urban League	Preriot	70	57	51	47
	Postriot	74	57	43	50
NAACP	Preriot	89	75	74	60
	Postriot	87	89	77	78
CORE	Preriot	36	26	27	17
	Postriot	13	19	12	10
SNCC	Preriot	15	15	10	9
	Postriot	4	11	4	0
Black Muslims	Preriot	2	5	5	4
	Postriot	0	2	1	0

[a] Percent favorable means percent "belonging to or would join" of total of that occupation responding.

Other Negro-rights organizations were not viewed as favorably as the NAACP (see Table 33). Generally, those with reputations for militancy were more negatively evaluated than the NAACP and were viewed even more negatively afterwards.

The effect of the riots on Negro attitudes toward Negro militancy seems to parallel the effect alleged about attitudes of whites. The findings about high interaction rates with whites would support this conclusion: those who interact more with whites might be expected to conform more to white views and reject militant organizations more strongly (as well as showing a slight tendency to less prejudice). The results, in part, confirm this collateral hypothesis. High rates of interaction with whites were significantly related to post-riot rejection of SNCC in the riot area and of CORE in the nonriot area.[7] Preriot rejection of SNCC and CORE for high interaction sets did not reach statistical significance. Pre- and postriot, riot area or nonriot area respondent sets all showed similar slight relations between high interaction with whites and rejection of Black Muslims.

We have claimed that the Urban League and NAACP are the more moderate organizations, and a high rate of inter-action with whites might be expected to show a positive relation with joining, or at least not a negative one. Espe-cially in the postriot period, these organizations, compared to more militant ones, might be more positively evaluated by Negroes who were in frequent interaction with whites. The Urban League was positively evaluated by those having high rates of interaction with whites in the nonriot area only, before but not after the riot.

Support of the NAACP shows no significant relation-ship with rate of interaction, in either direction, in any of the four possible combinations. This may reflect the phe-nomenon, noted previously, that the Negro support of NAACP varies mostly as to amount of neutrality after the riot. The Urban League and the NAACP are both more highly supported by white-collar workers than blue-collar, but the NAACP has proportionately greater white-collar sup-port than the Urban League. The difference in the number of people who give support may lie in this differential occupational structure, but we do not have sufficient cases for statistical tests.

Negro judgment that white fellow employees were

prejudiced showed little relation to support or rejection of any of the organizations. This "perceived prejudice" seems to be even less variable than any interaction factor following the riot, suggesting that the roots of prejudice are more related to the individual than to contemporary issues.

Proximity to the Riot

The rioting began in a congested commercial district adjacent to a public housing project, and looting and arson were mostly confined to that area and to two similar ones offering quick access via automobile. Each area was characterized by stores, small shops, bars, and adjacent relatively high-density housing. In such situations there is frequent personal contact, leading to possible crowd formation. Farther from such locations are the residential areas completing the total of nineteen census tracts in which Tampa's Negroes live. It might be expected that residents of areas distant from the riot locations would experience less of the excitement and encounter fewer of the conditions leading to crowd formation and hence participation. In this report, we are concerned with the consequences of rioting on opinion, rather than with riot participation itself. Those at a distance would be less likely to have personal contact with rioting action (see information above on visiting friends and relatives) but similar opportunity for exposure to mass media coverage of the event. Let us then trace the reasoning used previously about interaction, this time in regard to residential location. For operational purposes, the areas were divided into four sets of census tracts: primary riot area, secondary riot area, contiguous (to each of the riot areas), and outlying.

The postriot decrease in interaction with fellow employees away from work was statistically significant in the secondary riot area, and is close to significance in the primary area. In the outlying area, there is an increase in those who report both "much" and "little" talking. When tests are conducted by occupational status and by proximity to the riot area, no occupational status shows a significant change in interaction after the riot. Spatial analysis of the not-working in this regard is of course nonsensical since there is no interaction with employees, and a hypothetical analysis in this regard was not feasible. Considering only work and residential location, it seems likely that residential location is the more important factor in determining interaction relative to the riot.

We had no reason to predict that a tendency to talk with white coemployees would be related to residential location. It is surprising, then, that strong increases in talking with whites are reported by the secondary and outlying area respondents, with little change by respondents in the other areas. This seems partially to be due to the differential occupational structure of residents of the areas: both high blue-collar workers in the riot area and low blue-collar workers away from it show postriot increases. We can find no explanation for this. It should be recalled that the data on interaction is from the respondent's perception and not from objective measurement, and thus it is likely that there is extraneous material in the analysis.

Negro workers' perception of the prejudice of whites would be expected to be related in similar ways to work variables more than to residential location. As before, there are consistent minor decreases in perceived prejudice; however, the changes do not appear to be related specifically to the changes in interaction that were identified in related areas.

The only changes, in all four zones, in work satisfaction and personal happiness were slight decreases following the riot. In those areas where talk with fellow employees away from work diminished sharply and talk with white coworkers increased, the correlate was either decreased work satisfaction (outlying area) or decreased happiness (secondary area).

SUMMARY

The most striking conclusion concerning the effects of proximity appears not in the changes that took place, but in the lack of changes in the primary riot area. It must be emphasized that for a week this area was virtually under siege by a large force of police and national guardsmen. In terms of our research, the result of note: a minor decrease in reported conversation, and not much else!

This raises a salient question: Who is concerned about riots? Clearly civil authorities are, as are insurance underwriters, small retailers, absentee landlords, and any public that is interested in law and order. But our data suggest that people closest to riots are not concerned, or if they are, they show largely excitement or morbid interest. Riots, like the other transient dramatic events in the ghetto, are soon brought under control by outside forces and life becomes routine again.

What are the implications of these conclusions for our

findings about the social correlates of community voluntary association participation? Socially characterized, a riot is an episode of the temporary ascendance of mass man. Surely it is also an instance of the failure of routine social arrangements to bring change or to effect social control, and voluntary associations are among the intended instrumentalities to this end. Voluntary associations of Negroes, heavily dominated by white-collar workers, are oriented to social change to the benefit of Negroes in terms acceptable to white-collar workers. But the failure of the Negro community in general to join and strongly support the goals of the white-collar-dominated NAACP or Urban League, much less the more militant mass-oriented action groups, must give us pause.

NOTES

1. The data is from *United States Statistical Abstract*, 83d ed. We are not concerned here with the cause of the riot. Lieberson and Silverman present correlations on frequency of riots and city growth, proportion of Negroes, unemployment, and other items of interest. There is no reason to conclude that Tampa is weighted toward factors associated with prevalence of riots. It is interesting to note that the precipitating incident was typical of riots that occurred elsewhere in the U.S. the same summer. Lieberson and Silverman found that 15 percent of seventy-six riots between 1913 and 1963 were preceded by killing, arrest, interference, assault, or search of Negro men by white policemen. Stanley Lieberson and Arnold Silverman, "The Precipitants and Underlying Conditions of Race Riot," *American Sociological Review* 30, no. 6 (December 1965): 889.

2. The reader who wishes a more extensive background on

the riot and a comparison with other riots may consult the Kerner report (National Advisory Commission on Civil Disorders, *Report of the National Advisory Commission on Civil Disorders*).

3. Elihu Katz and Paul F. Lazarsfeld, *Personal Influence,* especially chapter 2.

4. A substantial proportion of the "members reported" membership in any organization is always a report of positive feeling, and not necessarily an accurate report of formal application and acceptance as the organization itself would see it. Hence immediate changes in reported membership might be found by researchers, but actual changes would be slower to materialize.

5. Katz and Lazarsfeld, *Personal Influence.*

6. J. R. Feagin, "Social Sources of Support for Violence and Nonviolence in a Negro Ghetto," *Social Problems* 15: 432–441.

7. This is suggested by the theory that relates interaction, norms, sentiments, and activity proposed by George Homans, *The Human Group.* We will not pursue this theory rigorously since we have no assurance that the necessary assumptions about the definition of a social system can be met in this research situation.

APPENDIXES
GLOSSARY
BIBLIOGRAPHY
INDEX

APPENDIX A

THE
INTERVIEW
SCHEDULE

The schedule is presented below. Details for the interviewer are edited. Page 1, with instructions to the interviewer, is omitted.

How many adults (between 20 and 60) in this dwelling have a job? None _____ One _____ Two or more _____

[If "none"] Then I need to interview the head of the house. Who is that? May I speak to him (her)? [If person is home, proceed to interview, starting with question #1. If not home, ask about best time to return *and note on page 1.*]

[If there is only one] Could I talk with him (her)?
[If person is home, proceed with interview, starting with question #1. If not home, ask about best time to return *and note on page 1.*]

[If there is more than one such person:] In order to decide who to interview, I have to list the people who work and then pick one. Who Works?: 1. _____
2. _____ 3. _____
[Proceed to interview the one of these who would conventionally be considered as head of the household, starting with question #1. If not home, ask about the best time to return *and note on page 1.*]

1. Now I would like to ask you about the people living here. How many people live here, including yourself and all children? _____ people

2. For each person living here, please tell me his relationship to you (such as daughter, son, father, friend, etc.) and each person's age. Let's start with you.

Relationship to respondent	Sex (M or F)	Age (approximate O.K.)

1. Respondent
[List any others on back of sheet. If you do so, check here _____.]
[Watch use of kinship terms as names.]

3. How many years have *you* lived at this address?
Less than 1, 1, 2, 3, 4, 5 or more

4. How many years has *this family* lived at this address?
Less than 1, 1, 2, 3, 4, 5 or more

5. Do you rent here or are you buying? Renting _____
Buying _____

6. Where did you live while you were growing up?
[If many places, when you were about 12?]
County _____
State _____

7. Was that: On a farm _____
In a small city _____ [specify name of
In a large city _____ city.]

8. What kind of work did your father do while you were
growing up? [Ask for specification of vague terms like
"self-employed," "working man," "in business," "white-
collar." If father unknown check here. _____]

9. [Ask only if respondent is female.] What kind of work
does your husband usually do? [Ask for specification
of vague terms, as above.]

10. Are you working now? Yes _____ No _____ [If
no, go to 13.]

11. Please briefly describe your work. [Ask for specification.]

12. Is this the kind of work you usually do? Yes _____
No _____ [If *no,* specify what the usual work is, and
go to question 15.]

13. [Ask only if "No" to question 10.] When was the
last time you worked? [Specify.]

14. [Ask only if "No" to question 10] What did you do?
[Specify.]

15. Do you work for a company, or a person, or are you
self-employed? [If not working now, ask about last
job.]

[If self-employed, check here _____ and go to question 27.]

[If person-employed, check here _____ and go to
question 21.]

[If company-employed, check here _____ and con-
tinue with question 16.]

16. What is the name of the Company? Name

17. About how many people work there? 1–5 6–10 11–20
    21–100 Over 100

18. Do you work with pretty much the same people all
    the time at work, or are there new people almost every
    week? Same _____ New _____

19. Is your direct supervisor (the person who tells you
    what to do) a Negro or a white? Negro _____
    White _____

20. [If white] Does he speak Spanish? Yes _____ No
    _____ Don't know _____ [If you asked question
    19, go to question 32.]

21. [Person-employed] Does the person you work for also
    hire anybody else? No _____ 1 other _____ 2–5
    _____ 6–10 _____ 11–12 _____ 21–100 _____
    100+ _____

22. Do you work with pretty much the same people all the
    time at work or are there new people almost every
    week? Same _____ New _____

23. Is your direct supervisor (the person who tells you
    what to do) a Negro or a White? Negro _____ White
    _____

24. [If white] Does he speak Spanish? Yes _____ No
    _____ Don't know _____

25. Do you work for more than one such employer in a
    week's time? Yes _____ No _____

26. [If "yes"] How many, usually? 2 3 4 5 6 7 8 9 or
    more
    [If you asked question 25, go to question 32.]

27. [Self-employed] Do you have any employees who work with you? Yes _____ No _____

28. [If "yes"] How many, usually? 1 2 3 4 5 6 7 8 9 or more

29. About how many customers (clients, etc.) Do you personally talk to in a typical day's work? None 1 2–5 6–10 11–100 100 or more

30. In your work, do you talk mostly to the same people over and over or do you mostly talk to new people all the time? Same _____ New _____ Some same, some new _____

31. Are the people you do work for (customers, clients, etc.) mostly Negroes, mostly whites, or what? Mostly Negroes _____ Mostly whites _____ Mixed _____ Other [describe:] _____

32. [Ask of all.] Do you usually work days, evenings, or nights? Days _____ Nights _____ Evenings _____ Other [Specify.] _____

33. Do many of your close friends work at the same place you work? None _____ Some, a few _____ Most, many _____

34. Do you talk to the people you work with away from work? [Decide which of the categories below best matches the answer.] No _____ Yes, sometimes _____ Yes, often _____ Yes, all the time _____

35. In the kind of work you do, do you work with other workers, or do you work alone most of the time? Alone _____ With others _____

36. [If "with others"] At work, do you have a chance to

talk with others about anything you want or do you
pretty much have to talk about work only? Work only
_____ Anything _____

37. [If work with others, also ask] Are those people you
work with mostly Negroes, or mostly whites? Negroes
_____ Whites _____ Mixed _____

38. [Ask of all] Do you get paid by the day, the week, every
two weeks, monthly, or how? Daily _____ Weekly
_____ Every two weeks _____ Monthly _____
Other [specify] _____

39. Do you usually get about the same amount of money
every week, or does it vary a lot from week to week?
Same _____ Varies _____

40. Do you belong to a union? Yes _____ No _____

41. [If "yes"] Which one? Name _____
Local number _____

42. Did you take any kind of examination in order to get
your job? No _____ Yes _____

43. [If "yes" to question 42] Was it a written examination?
Yes _____ No _____

44. [If "yes" to question 43] Could you tell me about it?
[Comment.]

45. Is your job under civil service? Yes _____ No _____
Don't know _____

46. Are there any whites working where you work (not
counting bosses)? Yes _____ No _____

47. [If "yes" to question 46] Do you ever talk with them
about things besides your work? [Classify answer as:]
Never _____ Sometimes _____ Often _____

48. [If "yes" to 46, also ask] Would you say that the whites where you work are very prejudiced, somewhat prejudiced, or not prejudiced against Negroes? Very _____ Somewhat _____ Not _____

49. All things considered, would you say that you are personally: Very happy _____ Fairly happy _____ Mostly unhappy _____ Very unhappy _____? [If no answer, add:] I have to mark one of these.

50. So far as your work is concerned, would you say you are very satisfied _____ Fairly satisfied _____ Unsatisfied _____ Very unsatisfied _____

51. If you had your choice right now, what kind of work would you like to be doing? [Specify.]

52. Right now, do you have definite plans to go into any different kind of work? Yes _____ No _____

53. [If "yes" to question 52] Could you tell me what kind of work that is?

Now I want to ask you some things about churches.

54. About how often do you go to church? [Classify answer as:] Once a week or more often _____ Two or three times a month _____ Once a month _____ Less than once a month _____ Never _____

55. Do you belong to a church? No _____ Yes _____

56. [If "yes" to question 55] What is the name of the church?
Name _____ City _____
[Be sure denomination is clear]

57. [If "yes" to question 55] Are you a member or do you

just sometimes go to that church? Member _____
Just go sometimes _____

58.   [Ask of all, whether church members or not] Thinking
      about the last Sunday morning that you attended church,
      did you know almost everyone there, about half, or were
      most strangers to you? Knew most _____ About half
      _____ Most strangers _____

You will find listed on this card [hand to respondent] a
number of organizations I want to ask you a few questions
about.

59.   Do you belong to any? [Ask of item 1 on card. For
      each "yes" answer, ask questions 60a through 60e. If
      respondent cannot read, offer to read them to him.]
      [As you ask about each type, make a check mark by it.]
          1. church groups (missionary societies, prayer bands,
             choir, Deacons, etc.)
          2. lodges—regular (Elks, Masons, Eastern Star, Odd-
             fellows, etc.)
          3. lodges—mutual-aid (Lilywhites, Grand Pallbearers
             Union, etc.)
          4. veterans' (VFW, American Legion, or auxiliaries)
          5. PTA
          6. local political clubs, such as ward clubs
          7. professional or business or service clubs, local or
             national
          8. sports and athletic clubs that meet regularly
          9. social groups, clubs, dance clubs, card clubs, etc.
         10. civil rights, such as NAACP, CORE, SNCC, etc.
         11. any others?

60a   What is the name of that organization? [List in table.]

60b If there is a branch, local, or lodge in that organization, which one is it? [List in table.]

60c Would you say that you go to meetings almost every time, about half the time, once in a while, or almost never? [List response in table.]

60d Were you ever an officer or on any regular committee? [Yes or no in table.]

60e Are there any other organizations of this type [Check type you are asking about] that you belong to? [If yes, go back through questions 60a–60d.]
[Be certain you ask about *every* item in question 59.]
[Organizational Membership Table—for answers to questions 59–60d]

59 *Group item*	60a *Name of organization*

60b *Branch?*	60c *Attendance*

60d *Office?*	

[If more organizations, list on back of page and check here _____.]

61. Now, does your wife (husband) belong to any of these kinds of organizations? No _____ Yes _____

62. [If "yes" to question 61] Just name them for me. [Simply write names.]

63. How often would you say you get together with relatives, friends, or neighbors (other than the ones who live in this place with you)? Would you say several times a week, once a week, once or twice a month, or less than once a month? [Read choices again.] Several times a week _____ Once a week _____ Once or twice a month _____ Less than once a month _____

64. [If not a member of NAACP, from table above:] Suppose you decided to join the NAACP, and the people you work with found out. What would they think of it? Approve _____ Not care _____ Not like it _____ [Record any comments.]

65. [If a member of NAACP, from table above:] Do the people you work with know you are a member of the NAACP? Yes _____ No _____

66. [If "yes" to question 65:] How do they feel about it? Doesn't matter _____ They approve _____ They disapprove _____

67. There are several national organizations working for Negro rights. Let me read you the names of some of them and I want you to tell me which ones you might join (or stay in) if you had the chance, which ones you feel rather undecided about, and which ones you would rather not join. The choices again are "would join," "undecided," "rather not join."

	Would Join or Belongs	Would Not Join Undecided
a. NAACP		
b. Black Muslims		
c. CORE		
d. Urban League		
e. SNCC ("snick")		

68. What was the highest year of school you completed? [Circle one.] 0 1 2 3 4 5 6 7 8 9 10 11 12 (high school grad.) 13 14 15 16 (college grad.) 17 or more.

69. What was the highest year of school of your wife (husband)? [Circle one.] 0 1 2 3 4 5 6 7 8 9 10 11 12 (high school grad.) 13 14 15 16 (college grad.) 17 or more.

70. What kind of meeting bothers you the most, one where nothing gets done or one where you don't enjoy the people you are with? Bothered when nothing gets done _____ Bothered when don't enjoy people _____ Other [specify] _____

[Quickly check to be certain all questions you should have asked are answered . . . do it now.]
[Thank the respondent for his time. Record below any comments you feel would be helpful in interpreting the answers.]

APPENDIX B

COLLATERAL
DATA

TABLE 34

PLACE RAISED BY OCCUPATIONAL STATUS[a]

OCCUPATIONAL STATUS	Rural %	Small City %	Large City %
White-collar	7	28	65
High blue-collar	13	41	45
Low blue-collar	13	39	48
Not working	11	42	46

[a] All row totals do not add to 100 percent due to rounding adjustments.

TABLE 35

OCCUPATIONAL STATUS AND FAMILY TYPE

OCCUPATIONAL STATUS	Nuclear %	Nuclear diminished[a] %	Other[b] %
White-collar	61	24	15
High blue-collar	75	12	13
Low blue-collar	52	31	17
Not working	26	56	18

[a] Nuclear diminished refers to occupation of a dwelling unit by a family with one less parent than is customary.
[b] "Other" consists of a variety of combinations of additions and subtractions relative to the nuclear family. Most common are: Nuclear diminished augmented (one parent missing, plus a related adult), nuclear augmented (parents and children, plus related adults, typically mother or father etc.), unrelated groups of friends (including one homosexual family), nuclear childless, and so on.

TABLE 36

NUMBER OF PERSONS IN HOUSEHOLD
BY OCCUPATIONAL STATUS (PERCENTS)[a]

OCCUPATIONAL STATUS	1	2	3	4	5	6+	N
White-collar	9	26	27	13	15	9	(149)
High blue-collar	4	23	15	18	12	28	(276)
Low blue-collar	10	20	20	15	12	22	(519)
Not working	11	24	10	17	9	28	(141)

[a] All row totals do not add to 100 percent due to rounding adjustments.

TABLE 37

AGE OF RESPONDENTS BY
OCCUPATIONAL STATUS (PERCENTS)[a]

| OCCUPATIONAL STATUS | YEARS | | | | Totals | |
	20–29	30–39	40–49	50–60	%	N
White-collar	21	27	28	24	100	(148)
High blue-collar	13	31	31	25	100	(273)
Low blue-collar	18	28	27	28	101	(517)
Not working	17	23	28	32	100	(141)

[a] Oldest age category is eleven years instead of ten.

TABLE 38

EDUCATION BY OCCUPATIONAL STATUS[a]

	YEARS OF EDUCATION				
OCCUPATIONAL STATUS	9 years or less %	10–11 years %	12 years or more %	Totals %	N
White-collar	18	12	70	100	(148)
High blue-collar	48	28	24	100	(277)
Low blue-collar	54	24	22	100	(518)
Not working	55	24	21	100	(141)

[a] The "12 years or more" column includes 48 college graduates who have white-collar occupations, and one in each of the other status categories.

TABLE 39

TIME OF WORK BY OCCUPATIONAL STATUS[a]

OCCUPATIONAL STATUS	Day %	Night %	Evening %	Other Combinations %	Total N
White-collar	73	2	2	23	(146)
High blue-collar	79	6	5	5	(275)
Low blue-collar	81	5	3	11	(515)
All working	79	5	2	14	(936)

[a] Evening refers to a time between day work and night work. See Appendix A for question wording.

TABLE 40

CORACIALISM AND WORK DAYS
ONLY BY OCCUPATIONAL STATUS (PERCENT)

OCCUPATIONAL STATUS	CORACIALISM		
	High	Medium	Low
White-collar	62 (88)[a]	82 (28)	93 (30)
High blue-collar	67 (21)	81 (164)	80 (164)
Low blue-collar	93 (30)	80 (90)	91 (190)

[a] Figures in parentheses refer to number of cases that percentages represent.

TABLE 41

PERSONAL HAPPINESS
BY OCCUPATIONAL STATUS

OCCUPATIONAL STATUS	Very happy	Less than very happy	Totals % N
White-collar	66 (95)[a]	34 (50)	100 (145)
High blue-collar	44 (121)	56 (152)	100 (273)
Low blue-collar	37 (188)	63 (317)	100 (505)

[a] Figures in parentheses refer to number of cases that percentages represent.

TABLE 42

WORK SATISFACTION
BY OCCUPATIONAL STATUS[a]

OCCUPATIONAL STATUS	Satisfied	Less Satisfied	Totals % N
White-collar	65 (94)[b]	35 (50)	100 (144)
High blue-collar	45 (122)	55 (151)	100 (273)
Low blue-collar	35 (178)	65 (327)	100 (505)
Not working	32 (30)	68 (64)	100 (94)

[a] The material is compiled from question 50. The original categories of response were: very satisfied, fairly satisfied, unsatisfied, very unsatisfied. Answers for those who were not working referred to the last time the person had worked.
[b] Figures in parentheses refer to number of cases that percentages represent.

TABLE 43

TALKS WITH WHITES AT WORK

	Never	Sometimes	Often	Total
N	89	380	202	671[a]
%	13	57	30	100

[a] Of the 1086 respondents, 274 working respondents did not acknowledge working with whites and 141 were not working.

TABLE 44

FREQUENCY OF VISITING RELATIVES, FRIENDS, OR NEIGHBORS BY STATUS

OCCUPATIONAL STATUS	More than once a week	Once a week	Once or twice a month	Once a month or less	Totals % N
White-collar	32 (47)[a]	28 (42)	18 (27)	22 (22)	100 (148)
High blue-collar	30 (83)	28 (76)	25 (70)	17 (47)	100 (276)
Low blue-collar	34 (175)	22 (116)	22 (111)	22 (115)	100 (517)
Not working	35 (49)	15 (21)	22 (31)	28 (40)	100 (141)
All occupations	33 (354)	23 (255)	22 (239)	22 (234)	100 (1,082)

[a] Figures in parentheses refer to number of cases which percentages represent.

TABLE 45

EXPECTED FELLOW EMPLOYEES' REACTIONS TO HYPOTHETICAL
MEMBERSHIP IN NAACP (FOR NONMEMBERS)

OCCUPATIONAL STATUS	Approve	Doesn't matter	Disapprove	Totals % N
White-collar	57 (46)[a]	39 (31)	4 (3)	100 (80)
High blue-collar	78 (178)	9 (21)	12 (28)	100 (227)
Low blue-collar	75 (300)	15 (60)	10 (40)	100 (400)
Not working[b]	69 (51)	20 (15)	11 (8)	100 (74)

[a] Figures in parentheses refer to number of cases parentheses represent.
[b] Refers to situation when working.

TABLE 46

FELLOW EMPLOYEES' REACTIONS TO ACTUAL
MEMBERSHIP IN NAACP BY STATUS

OCCUPATIONAL STATUS	Approve	Doesn't matter	Dis-approve	Unaware	Total
White-collar	28	12	2	9	51
High blue-collar	2	3	2	7	14
Low blue-collar	4	14	1	18	37
Not working[a]	0	1	0	2	3
Total	34	30	5	36	105

[a] Refers to situation when working.

GLOSSARY

The items included here are those concepts that are original in this study and are frequently used as an integral part of the research. Concepts in common sociological parlance that have been given a restricted definition are also included.

Authority. Legitimated ability to obtain compliance.

Collegiality. Work-related friendship.

Company-employed. Status of those working for a company or corporate firm or bureaucratic organization, whether or not for profit.

Coracialism. Work with other Negroes.

Emploity. Institutionalization of control mechanisms concerning work and workers integrated with the normative structure of plural organizations or groups.

Expressive voluntary association. A voluntary association in which membership is meaningful by virtue of the value to the member of engaging in interaction with other members.

Extensivity. Multiple membership spanning more than one kind of voluntary association.

High blue-collar. Status of those working at jobs classified as skilled and semiskilled, or craftsmen and operatives.

Instrumental voluntary association. (Following Gordon and Babchuk) a voluntary association serving as a social influence organization designed to maintain or to create some normative condition change.

Intensivity. Multiple membership in one kind of voluntary association.

Low blue-collar. Status of those working at jobs classified as unskilled or manual.

Mass society. (Following Kornhauser) a social system in which elites are accessible to influence by nonelites and nonelites are readily accessible to influence by elites.

Occupational community. A form of community articulated about a particular emploity.

Person-employed. Status of those working for a single person or entrepreneur.

Phase segregation. A regular or systematic disjunction of persons and communities, involving mismatching of cycles or rhythms of those who work while the community does not.

Pluralist society. (Following Kornhauser) a social system characterized by the low availability of nonelites and high availability of elites.

Reinforcement. The worker's ability to call upon extrasystemic force in work.

Self-employed. Status of those who habitually contract for their own work, obtain their living by seeking clients, and have a high degree of responsibility for the success or failure of their own enterprises.

Specialization. Participation exclusively in one voluntary association.

Statistical significance. Condition when a statistical test has been performed and the given result could not have occurred five or more times out of a hundred by chance alone.

Type of employer. An operational classification of employers as self, person, or company (defined elsewhere in glossary) according to respondent's report.

Voluntary association. A formal organization, small or large, in which membership is optional; that is, without compulsion or ascription.

White-collar. Status of those working at jobs classified as clerical and sales; managers, proprietors, and officials; professional, technical, and kindred.

Work imperialism. The organization of work into time units under strong authority such that completion of a work sequence is imperative regardless of its situation in time or space.

BIBLIOGRAPHY

Babchuk, Nicholas, and Gordon, C. Wayne. *The Voluntary Association in the Slum.* Lincoln, Nebraska: University of Nebraska Press, 1962.

Babchuk, Nicholas, and Thompson, Ralph V. "Voluntary Associations of Negroes." *American Sociological Review* 27:647–655.

Bell, Inge Powell. *CORE and the Strategy of Non-Violence.* New York: Random House, 1968.

Billingsley, Andrew. *Black Families in White America.* Englewood Cliffs, N.J: Prentice-Hall, 1968.

Blalock, Hubert M., Jr. *Toward a Theory of Minority-Group Relations.* New York: John Wiley & Sons, 1967.

Blum, Fred. *Toward a Democratic Work Process.* New York: Harper & Brothers, 1953.

Blumenthal, Albert. *Small Town Stuff.* Chicago: University of Chicago Press, 1932.

Booth, Alan James. "Personal Influence on the Decision to Join Voluntary Associations." Ph.D. thesis, University of Nebraska, 1966.

————. "Personal Influence and the Decision to Participate in Voluntary Associations." Paper presented at the 1966 Meeting of the American Sociological Association.

Breed, Warren. "Group Structure and Resistance to Desegregation in the Deep South." *Social Problems* 10:84–94.

Cameron, W. B. *Informal Sociology*. New York: Random House, 1963.

Cauter, Thomas, and Downham, John S. *The Communication of Ideas*. London: Chatto and Windus, 1954.

Chaplin, David. "Domestic Service and the Negro." *Blue-Collar World: Studies of the American Worker,* edited by Arthur B. Shostak and William Gomberg. Englewood Cliffs, N.J.: Prentice-Hall, 1964.

Collins, Orvis. "Ethnic Behavior in Industry: Sponsorship and Rejection in a New England Factory." *American Journal of Sociology* 51:293–298.

Cottrell, W. F. "Of Time and the Railroader." *American Sociological Review* 4:190–198.

————. The Railroader. Stanford: Stanford University Press, 1940.

Dewey, Donald. "Negro Employment in Southern Industry." *Journal of Political Economy* 60:279–293.

Downham, John S. *The Communication of Ideas*. London: Chatto and Windus, 1954.

Drake, St. Clair, and Cayton, Horace R. *Black Metropolis*. 2 vols. New York: Harcourt, Brace, and Co., 1945.

Durant, Ruth. *Watling*. London: King, 1939.

Essien-Udom, E. U. *Black Nationalism.* New York: Dell Publishing Co., 1962.

Feagin, J. R. "Social Sources of Support for Violence and Nonviolence in a Negro Ghetto." *Social Problems* 15:432–441.

Ferguson, Charles W. *Fifty Million Brothers.* New York: Farrar and Rinehart, 1937.

Ferman, Louis A.; Kornbluh, Joyce L.; and Miller, J. A. *Negroes and Jobs: A Book of Readings.* Ann Arbor: University of Michigan Press, 1968.

Florida Sentinel-Bulletin, Tampa, Florida.

Frazier, E. Franklin. *Black Bourgeoisie.* New York: Collier Books, 1962.

————. *The Negro Church in America.* New York: Schocken Books, 1964.

Gordon, C. Wayne, and Babchuk, Nicholas. "A Typology of Voluntary Associations." *American Sociological Review* 24: 22–29.

Greer, Scott. *Last Man In.* New York: Free Press of Glencoe, 1959.

Hall, M. Penelope. *Community Centers and Associations in Manchester.* Manchester, England: Manchester and Salford Councils of Social Service, 1946.

Hausknecht, Murray. *The Joiners: A Sociological Description of Voluntary Association Membership in the United States.* New York: Bedminster Press, 1962.

Hodge, Robert W., and Treiman, Donald J. "Social Participation and Social Status." *American Sociological Review* 33: 722–740.

Hollingshead, August B. *Elmtown's Youth.* New York: John Wiley & Sons, 1949.

Homans, George. *The Human Group*. New York: Harcourt, Brace, and Co., 1950.

Hughes, Everett C. "Race Relations in Industry." *Industry and Society*, edited by William Foote Whyte. New York: McGraw-Hill, 1946.

──────. "Queries Concerning Industry and Society Growing Out of Study of Ethnic Relations in Industry." *American Sociological Review* 14:211–220.

Hughes, Langston. *Fight For Freedom: The Story of the NAACP*. New York: W. W. Norton & Co., 1962.

Katz, Elihu, and Lazarsfeld, Paul F. *Personal Influence*. Glencoe, Ill.: Free Press, 1955.

Keil, Charles. *Urban Blues*. Chicago: University of Chicago Press, 1966.

King, Martin Luther, Jr. *Strength to Love*. New York: Harper & Row, 1963.

──────. *Stride Toward Freedom*. New York: Harper & Brothers, 1958.

──────. *Where Do We Go From Here: Chaos or Community*. New York: Harper & Row, 1967.

──────. *Why We Can't Wait*. New York: Harper & Row, 1963.

Kornhauser, William. *The Politics of Mass Society*. Glencoe, Ill.: Free Press, 1959.

Lenski, Gerhard. *The Religious Factor*. Rev. ed. Garden City, N.Y.: Doubleday & Co., 1963.

Lewis, Hylan. *Blackways of Kent*. New Haven: College and University Press, 1964.

Liebow, Elliot. *Tally's Corner: A Study of Negro Streetcorner Men*. Boston: Little, Brown, and Co., 1967.

Lincoln, Eric. *The Black Muslims in America.* Boston: Beacon Press, 1961.

Lipset, Seymour M., Trow, Martin, and Coleman, J. S. *Union Democracy.* Glencoe, Ill.: Free Press, 1956.

Litwak, Eugene. "Voluntary Associations and Neighborhood Cohesion." *American Sociological Review* 26:258–271.

Lomax, Louis E. *When the Word is Given.* New York: Signet Books, 1963.

Lopata, Helena Z. "The Functions of Voluntary Associations in an Ethnic Community: 'Polonia'." *Contributions to Urban Sociology,* edited by Ernest W. Burgess and Donald J. Bogue. Chicago: University of Chicago Press, 1964.

Lynd, Robert S., and Lynd, Helen Merrell. *Middletown,* New York: Harcourt, Brace, and Co., 1929.

———. *Middletown in Transition.* New York: Harcourt, Brace, and World, 1937.

Marx, Gary. *Protest and Prejudice.* New York: Harper & Row, 1967.

Matza, David. "Poverty and Disrepute." *Contemporary Social Problems,* 2d ed., edited by Robert K. Merton and Robert A. Nisbet. New York: Harcourt, Brace, and World, 1966.

Mills, C. Wright. *White Collar.* New York: Oxford University Press, 1951.

Mizruchi, Ephraim H. *Success and Opportunity.* London: Free Press of Glencoe, 1964.

Myers, Richard R. "Interpersonal Relations in the Building Industry." *Man, Work, and Society,* edited by Sigmund Nosow, and William H. Form. New York: Basic Books, 1962.

Myrdal, Gunnar, with the assistance of Richard Sterner and Arnold Rose. *An American Dilemma.* 2 vols. New York: McGraw-Hill, 1964.

National Advisory Commission on Civil Disorders. *Report of the National Advisory Commission on Civil Disorders.* Washington, D.C.: Government Printing Office, 1968.

Newfield, Jack. *A Prophetic Minority.* New York: New American Library, 1966.

Parsons, Talcott. *The Social System.* Glencoe, Ill.: Free Press, 1951.

Pellegrin, Roland J., and Coates, Charles H. "Absentee-Owned Corporations and Community Power Structure." *American Journal of Sociology* 61:413–419.

Reitzes, Dietrich C. "Union vs. Neighborhood in a Tension Situation." *Racial and Ethnic Relations,* edited by Bernard L. Segal. New York: Thomas Y. Crowell Co., 1966.

Robertson, D. B., ed. *Voluntary Associations, A Study of Groups in Free Societies: Essays in Honor of James Luther Adams.* Richmond, Va.: John Knox Press, 1966.

Roper Power, Edward R. "The Social Structure of an English Country Town." *Sociological Review* 29:391–413.

Rose, Arnold M. *The Power Structure.* New York: Oxford University Press, 1967.

————. *Theory and Method in the Social Sciences.* Minneapolis: University of Minnesota Press, 1954.

Ross, Aileen. "Philanthropic Activity in the Business Career." *Man, Work, and Society,* edited by Sigmund Nosow and William H. Form. New York: Basic Books, 1962.

Ross, Jack C., and Wheeler, Raymond. "Structural Sources of Threat to Negro Membership in Voluntary Associations in a Southern City." *Social Forces* 45:583–586.

Rossi, Peter. "Voluntary Associations in an Industrial City." *The Government of Associations,* edited by William A. Glaser and

David L. Sills. Totowa, New Jersey: The Bedminster Press, 1966.

Sills, David L. *The Volunteers: Means and Ends in a National Organization*. Glencoe, Ill.: Free Press, 1957.

Spinrad, William. "Correlates of Trade Union Participation." *American Sociological Review* 25:237–244.

Tocqueville, Alexis de. *Democracy in America*. New York: Mentor Books, 1956.

Troeltsch, Ernst. *Social Teachings of the Christian Churches*. 2 vols. New York: Harper & Brothers, 1960.

United States Statistical Abstract. 83d ed. Washington, D.C.: Government Printing Office, 1962.

Warner, W. Lloyd, et al. *Democracy in Jonesville: A Study in Quality and Inequality*. New York: Harper & Brothers, 1949.

Warner, W. Lloyd, and Low, J. O. *The Social System of the Modern Factory*. New Haven: Yale University Press, 1947.

Warner, W. Lloyd, and Lunt, Paul S. *The Social Life of a Modern Community*. New Haven: Yale University Press, 1941.

Warner, W. Lloyd; Meeker, Marchia; and Eells, Kenneth. *Social Class in America: A Manual of Procedure for the Measurement of Social Status*. New York: Harper & Row, 1960.

Warriner, Charles, and Prather, Jane Emery. "Four Types of Voluntary Associations." *Sociological Inquiry* 35:138–148.

Washington, Joseph R., Jr. *Black Religion: The Negro and Christianity in the United States*. Boston: Beacon Press, 1964.

Whyte, William H., Jr. *The Organization Man*. Garden City, N.Y.: Doubleday Anchor Books, 1956.

Williams, Robin M., Jr. *Strangers Next Door: Ethnic Relations in American Communities*. Englewood Cliffs, N.J.: Prentice-Hall, 1964.

Wilson, Bryon. "An Analysis of Sect Development." *American Sociological Review* 24:3–15.

Wright, Charles R., and Hyman, Herbert H. "Voluntary Association Memberships of American Adults: Evidence from National Samples." *American Sociological Review* 23:284–294.

Yinger, J. Milton. *Religion, Society, and the Individual.* New York: The Macmillan Co., 1957.

Young, Terence. *Beacontree and Dagenham.* London: Pilgrim Trust, 1934.

Young, Whitney. *To Be Equal.* New York: McGraw-Hill, 1964.

Zinn, Howard. *SNCC: The New Abolitionists.* Boston: Beacon Press, 1964.

INDEX

age, 22, 62, 63

African Methodist Episcopal, 106

alienation: in Civil Service, 29; and mass production, 17; in Negro school, 49n; of supervisors, 17; of unskilled and unemployed, 56

American dream, 18

American Federation of Teachers, 149

Americans, 11

anomie, 140n

ascriptive, criteria of voluntarism, 136n

associations, 4, 10, 24, 39, 51n

attendance: causes of low frequency of, 35; and church, 124, 205, 208, 234, 236; correlates of 142; at cult, 208; by expressive vs. instrumental, 134; in expressive VA, 134; of multiple joiners, 128; at mutual-aid lodges, 125; at Negro-rights VA, 125; patterns of, 165; at professional VA, 124–125; at PTA, 124–125; ratio of to membership, 125; at veterans' VA, 124

attitudes: and collegiality, 180; and coracialism, 180; and joining data, 185; definition of, 179; postriot VA, 237; and reinforcement, 180; as research variables, 178, 180; and status, 180

attorney, 25

authority: alienating, 15; blue-collar, 18, 26; in bureaucracy, 24; in "church," 204; concept of, 37; conflict with reinforcement, 26; as contractual, 13; in coracialism index, 42; definition of, 12, 97; and domestics, 15; of employers, 14, 77, 142; and entrepreneur, 27; operationalized, 47n; and operatives, 20; and personal relations, 21; of white supervisor, 42; and worker, 13

194*n*; Cubans in, 104; domestics
in, 48*n*; hiring hall in, 29; industry in, 17; as mass society, 10;
migrants in, 63; NAACP in, 174;
Negro in, 9, 10, 20, 21, 34, 40,
162, 175, 187, 219, 220*n*, 226;
and research, 4, 41; and riot of
1967, 42, 117–118, 224–225,
243*n*; school types in, 128; SNCC
in, 194*n*; social tendencies in, 11;
Spanish groups in, 103; Urban
League in, 174; VA in, 103; work
patterns, 129
task, 19; differentiation of, 17
teachers: in "church," 213; coracialism of, 75, 152; in cults, 213;
as degree holders, 75; in denomination, 213; in established sect,
213; as large organization employees, 76, 152–153; as leaders,
128; limits of employment, 25;
militance of, 75; and Negro supervisors, 75; and PTA, 12; and
residence length, 75; as salaried,
75; and VA approved, 111, 174,
193*n*
tests, of significance, 89*n*, 90*n*
theory: approach of study, 4; basic
aspects of, 74; on collegiality, 150;
and community studies, 5; on
coracialism, 71; distinctions as to
VA forms, 100; final, 36; formation of, 37; and high blue-collar,
177–178; on interaction, 244*n*;
made practical, 42; mass society
concept in, 10; of Negro participation, 9; occupational status in,
15; part of status in, 70–71; problem statement, 11; provisional,
11; and source of extraneous data,
58; and status, 59; tests reviewed,
174
type of employment: and authority,
77, 142; cateogries listed, 77;
class bias of, 80; composition of
category, 153; correlates reviewed,
142; of low blue-collar, 159; and
male heads of household, 85; and

membership, 81; operationalizing,
77; and pluralism summary, 84;
see also employment

unemployed: and emploity, 163; and
high blue-collar, 58; and low
blue-collar, 58; and social relations, 163; and social workers, 14;
and unskilled, 56, 58; VA rates
of, 56; and white-collar, 58, 167*n*
unemployment, 14, 16, 162
union: analysis of, 197, 198; and
associations, 8, 39; and collegiality,
157; among company-employed,
218; female membership of, 217;
and high blue-collar joining, 157;
and instrumental VA, 219; and
isolated workers, 218; and joining,
216; of longshoremen, 162; and
low blue-collar, 218; male membership of, 217; membership in,
8, 55, 198, 216; and NAACP
membership, 214; Negro membership of, 39, 218; and Negro-
rights VA, 38; as nonvoluntary
association, 4, 8, 55, 98, 215; and
not-working, 162, 216–217;
occupational community of, 26, 30,
193*n*; and participation and VA,
39; particularistic joining, 216;
race attitudes in, 50*n*; racial composition of, 30; as reinforcement,
17, 21, 38, 39, 43, 198, 216;
and security of skilled Negroes,
193*n*; and SNCC, 188, 218; and
status distribution, 216; in theory
formation, 8; and white-collar,
149; and work, 8, 49*n*
United States Office of Economic
Opportunity, 29
unskilled workers: hiring of, 34;
on status scale, 56; and unemployed, 56, 58
urbanization, 64
Urban League: approval of, 186;
attitudes and social relations of,
184; and church members, 192,
214; and conservation, 195*n*;

Index

action, 239; membership data of,
181; and NAACP, 175, 185, 187;
as Negro-rights organization, 117;
postriot status of, 239; programs
of, 175; and riot, 243; strength of,
175; white-collar in, 194n, 239;
and whites, 185

values: of employee, 28; on participation, 40; in professional work,
27; in riot, 229, 236; universalistic
work standards, 24; of VA, 97
veterans VA, 102; attendance of,
125; as church members, 123; as
expressive, 133; as membership
proportion, 109; national links of,
172; among Negroes, 108–109;
officers as, 130–131; as permanent
organization, 131
voluntarism, and free church, 204
voluntary association (VA): age
and, 42, 63; of Americans, 11,
134n; and attendance, 33, 35,
124–125, 205–206; attitudes
toward, 179; of black bourgeoisie,
137n; of blue-collar, 154; and
business, 8, 22; causes of joining
reviewed, 141; and church, 40,
102, 106, 119, 122, 123, 133, 134,
149, 152, 154, 159–160, 166n,
211; and charisma, 117; and collegiality of bureaucratic professionals, 25, 149–150, 157, 190;
and common interest, 97; and
company-employed, 80, 154; and
community study, 5, 44n, 46n;
and coracialism, 72, 74, 143, 148,
155–156, 160; defined, 3–4, 6, 96–
97; denominations, 209; economic
enterprise and membership, 8;
and education, 58–59; eleemosynary, 97; and established sects,
209; expressive, see expressive VA;
as a family, 8; and family life
cycle, 63, 90n, 138n; function
of, 5; and goal attainment, 99;
and high blue-collar, 91n, 155–

156; in hypothesis, 36–37; as
institutions, 169; instrumental, see
instrumental VA; leisure alternatives to, 33; and linkages, 174;
and low blue-collar, 158–159, 218;
membership of, xi, 3, 6, 26, 35,
37–38, 53, 55, 91n, 118–119, 150;
and multiple membership, 121–
122; and national organizations,
25; of Negroes, 9, 26, 47n, 114;
and Negro-rights, 170; and Negro
supervision, 67; of nonprofessional, 151; and non-work factors,
85; norms and, 19; not-working
members, 14, 161–163; and occupations, xi, 7; organizational
problems, 99; and other organizations, 97; in occupational community, 31, 193n; and participation, 6, 35; and phase segregation,
33; pluralism, 119; and polity, 7;
and power structure, 47n; and
productivity, 97; of professionals,
23, 25; and race, 170; reinforcement and, 38; research on, 6–8,
19, 65; residence length, 62; in
riot, 230, 243; self-employed
Negroes in, 10; and sex, 92n; and
shop members, 90n; as social
investment capital, 90n; and social
class, 6–7; and social relations
variables, 45n, 85; in society, 5;
in sociology, 5; and status, xi,
6–7, 55–56, 144, 172; as study
focus, 7; in Tampa, 103; theory
of, 5, 36; types of, 95, 98, 100–
103, 125, 130, 167n, 170; of
typographers, 31; and union, 39,
215; uniqueness of, 169; and
Urban League joining, 186; and
visiting patterns, 86–87; and
welfare recipients, 164; and white-
collar, 85; of whites, 9, 114; and
work imperialism, 33; and work,
3, 7–8, 12, 33; see also organization; association

welfare, 14, 163, 164

DATE DUE